The Perfection of Everything

A Recovery Memoir

2nd Ed.

Mountain Page Press
Hendersonville, NC

Copyright © 2016, 2021 by Ali Webster

All rights reserved. This book or any portion thereof may not be reproduced or used in any manner whatsoever without the express written permission of the author except for the use of brief quotations in a book review.

Some names and identifying details have been changed to protect the privacy of individuals.

"The Perfection of Everything: A Recovery Memoir"

2nd Ed.

Mountain Page Press
118 5th Ave. W.
Hendersonville, NC 28792

Printed in the United States
Published by Mountain Page Press
Cover photo by Derek Baron

ISBN-978-1-952714-24-5

First printing, 2016
2nd Edition published 2019, 2021

Additional copies can be ordered through
www.amazon.com or www.MountainPagePress.com

Dedication

To Abby without whom I might not be.

And to my Mom, Pat Webster, who is sooooooo opossum!

Table of Contents

The Perfection of Everything	I
Dedication	III
Introduction: Saved	i
Bookend One	1
Death	7
The Light: My Mom	13
Mom and the Fair	19
Caterpillar	25
Or, Who I want to Be	25
Reason, Season or Lifetime	29
Sobriety and Kindness: My Bottom	37
The Day I Decided to Reboot	45
Solo	51
Whirlwind, Ramana's Garden	55
Baggage and God	67
Christmas Safari	73
Differences	79
Shiva Temple	83
Steam Room	95
Recovery Table	99
Blackbird	107
Bath	111
David	115
Nepal Versus Now	121
The Perfection of Everything	127
Goodbye	131
Gigi's Funeral	137
Trish	141
Bookend Two	149
About the Author	153

Introduction: Saved

I remember when I was saved like it was yesterday.

It happened at a Rick Scarborough revival and I trudged all the way from the back of the auditorium, at age eight, to the stage, alone. Well, with Jesus. They had asked us, quite nicely, to allow him in our hearts, and I had. He was there and I wanted to take care of him. Something was kindled, not so much something new being born, but rather something that was always there being re-ignited, re-highlighted in belief. Known as real.

Later that night, I was in a strange family member's guest room, staring at the walls. They were covered in this wood paneling, thin strips of plywood. I prayed, said hello to my heart, to the feeling of God there: a very real, glowing warmth, a tingly bursting. That wood paneling rippled with varying lines of brown, light tan and dark mahogany. And I saw the face of what I imagined Jesus to look like in those ripples. Or maybe it was just that I could access the truth in that moment, that Jesus's face is in everything. I have come to believe that awareness encompasses the All, the More, the Universal Divine.

Whatever path takes one to the Divine is fine by me. I have been led by the hand of Krishna, Native American wisdom, gurus, yogis, Babas and Buddhists. It doesn't matter where the wisdom lies or what colors it is painted with, life is sacred and driven by something more, and where that is concerned, I am all in. For many years I lost that connection; it was as if I had a phone line that was damaged, the signal scratchy, my apparatus inadequate. Now, in sobriety, I am ready to listen again.

BOOKEND ONE

My cousin Aaron was in New York. He was chosen to be on that illustrious venue of new, holy restaurant business acclaims, The Food Network. He was pushing our family's Southern style of food love in his own, uniquely artful way on a twenty-four-hour restaurant battle show. We were celebrating. He'd come by my restaurant with his partner the night before entering a secret lockdown, a four-day-long filming process. I was proud to bask in his golden glow, drips of his eminent effigy scattered upon my head, somehow making my insane choice of becoming a general manager of this downtown Manhattan bistro more sane, even admirable.

We drank red wine and it made everything fine. I took him to my favorite star chef and former coworker, Marc Murphy's cool little downtown bistro, LandMarc to show off. We drank bottles of vino. Johann, my head server and sometimes assistant manager, was there. Something happened with my pants and now I smelled bad. The rest of the night was a brown-out in my brain; bits and pieces, little splotches of incomplete moments, like us sitting and eating at Bubby's, a famous Jewish, post-drinking diner and hot spot.

Or before we ate at Bubby's, when we had to stand in line outside, with all of the other 3:00 am NY city partiers, hungry and in need of grease to soak up the booze. That memory is spotted, coming through in broken pieces, not quite real, like a too vivid dream.

But wait, was that part of it? Was that real? That fuzzy brown-out, semi-real memory where I am horizontal on the sidewalk and somehow the stanchion—that big heavy metal pole which strings together red velvet ropes—is on top of me.

Every alcoholic knows this type of memory where events don't make any sense. Sometimes they are too real, sometimes too easy to push off into the recesses of forgettable and hopefully not real potential imaginings. The heavy part of the stanchion feels like it hit me on the butt, but how did it get off the ground? Wait, I catch a memory glimpse of me, drunken and wobbly, falling against the ropes and pulling it down. Was that a real memory?

It must have been because I wake in the morning (where did morning come from?) with a bruise the size of Texas on my right hip. I didn't know the body could do that. It is as dark and menacing as a blood blister, but at least a foot long and stony hard, with marbling variations of purple-black and it's raised a good inch or so off my flesh. It feels deathly.

I am in the shower. I am stretching my calves. Years of working on my feet have given me plantar fasciitis and a heel spur so that sometimes walking does not seem remotely possible because of the searing pain. My brilliant, kind, gift from God podiatrist had told me reluctantly, in all earnestness, that although he would profit more from prescribing surgeries and drugs, he has found that these simple stretches can cure even thwarted disabled runners who return to running after many years of inactivity. He said to stretch the calves three times a day. I do it only once, in the shower.

It is like this little crack of self-love and caretaking has opened some barrier to some other side. As light pours in through a crevice; it is blinding in its contrast to where I am now, in the dark, nursing the bruise from hell and trying to recall the events of the night before, again.

More memories bubble to the surface from last night. Having been stopped by the supervisor, Milan, as has frequently become my ritual, I staggered into my building on Crescent Street in Astoria. He saw me stumbling home from the train, released into a deep puddle from a cab and asked me how my night was, eventually luring me into his lair, a little office in the basement, probably a boiler room.

I'm not sure of any of this. In that boiler room/office odd energy lingers like bad cobwebs from tenants gone. It seeps out of shadows in that creepy, barely lit cement tomb, paintings left behind leaning against the gray, cinder block formed walls, bicycles in various phases of disrepair, boxes holding unknown treasures and secrets. He offers me red wine and cigarettes.

Just what I need at these moments, huh? We smoke and talk and drink or rather he talks and I listen, swaying on the chair and trying to discern when I can leave this place.

He tried to kiss me once, after helping me cut my Christmas tree into pieces with a saw to get it out of my apartment without trailing prodigious pine needles; the neighbors had complained that I still had it up, a dry fire hazard. I was embarrassed. I usually left it up until Valentine's Day as was my mother's and my custom, something sweet to linger from Christmas, our favorite holiday. That secret lingers as a weird glue between us, neither ever mentioning nor forgetting it.

In the shower, the fact that I have been smoking cigarettes at all hits me like an anvil of self-mutilation, the weight of it all of a sudden, too loathsome to bear. I remember being a child at my dad's house and forced to use a gas mask while he smoked cigarettes by the television because I got sore throats after visits to his house. How could I consciously choose to do that to myself after having hated it so much and having quit for a year and a half?!

Then all the other jarring incidents I had allowed, or even just witnessed in my now seemingly epic lifetime of torture from without and from within, start reeling through my weary, hungover brain, playing like bad scenes in a horror film: molestation and inappropriate parental behavior; a friend's father touching me in the sink, playing doctor, aiding with a supposed boo-boo, something that should not happen with any child; my mom's hippy friends parading around naked and playing a game called, "Where is the Rubber Ring?" in a hot tub with their penises as the winning landing spot; babysitters torturing me with tales of the end of the world while forcing two naked twins to sixty-nine on a rug in front of me while Mom is having a nervous breakdown with her friend Norma in another apartment.

It may sound like I am sweeping all of this under the rug, but these experiences created in me an ever growing spirit of independence. A character trait that both served me well and drove me into the corners of insanity.

And then the other horrors: date rapes; bad choices; a career as a professional bus baby—a term a shrink in Los Angeles coined for my codependent servitude to my mother as a child. Doing drugs, going to scary neighborhoods, riding trains and getting lost in the middle of the night in both Los Angeles and New York. Years of the worst kind of craziness. It hits me in a cascade of clarity how much I have hurt myself. And, still in the shower, I start to cry. I can't stop; it's as if a dam broke and tons of unleashed water is battering my worn-down psyche with the power of the Ganges River. I finally get ready for work while the tears are still coming.

I ride the train and they are trickling now. I have never cried about these things because I had to be strong. Working the lunch shift, I barely hold it together, hiding while sorting through the checkout reports in the coffee station corner and never visiting the tables once. Staff stays away from me.

After lunch, I walk to the clinic; tears boiling out again as I pass Trinity Church, remembering another drunken night where my alcoholic ex Sean and I tried to break in…a vague and powerful memory.

In the clinic, a nurse swoops to my rescue and takes me back to a room to let me cry. She tells me to take as long as I need, that I am not about to have a blood clot-induced stroke, that it is just a very bad bruise and the fever I have is just dehydration from so many tears. I cry into the phone to my shrink, call Johann to cover the restaurant for the rest of the day, and go home to finish this complete and utter breakdown. Little did I know it then, but that was the necessary beginning of my journey to recovery.

Death

There was something heavy in the air, the disquiet of something missing. The glittery specks of dust floating in the faded light of that old wooden house seemed more dispersed, their interstices more pronounced.

Mom says my little four-year-old form went up to her on tiptoes in my tiny white socks, then crawled up on her lap where she waited in that old squeak-and-hush rocking chair and, with apprehension, began asking her the following questions:

"Mama, is Gamy (her mother) bwoke?"

She began rocking my tiny form back and forth and answered, "No, Ali, Gamy isn't broke."

"Is Nat bwoke?" I inquired tentatively about my uncle.

"No, Ali, Nat's not broke."

Quiet. Long pause. "Is Mom bwoke?"

"No, Ali, Mom's not broke."

And, after the longest pause, the hardest question of all made its way through my trembling lips. "Is Ali bwoke?"

She smiled and rocked and said, "No, Ali is not broke."

After a moment of understanding, the truth came out of my own mouth, "Bwuce Bwoke."

"Yes, Ali, Bruce is broke."

In my two-story, yellow, wooden childhood house with its seven cats and several roommates to supplement my single working-mother's income, one of them had died. It was a bad car accident, and his sudden absence at the time had threatened the very fabric of my being. But once the fundamentals had been reestablished, I sensed that, though there was sadness, all was still right with the world.

That sense of order and perfection has stayed with me, knowing that deep down, underneath it all, below the river of illusion where we live day-to-day, in the flow of chaos and interruption, in frequent confusion and misdirection, under all of it, is perfection. The muddy, labyrinthine root of truth that all is well with the Universe, all the time.

As I grew older, I began to take part in some Native American rituals, assisting my mom in leading workshops with vision quests, sweats and medicine circles (as she was taught by a shaman named Gray Antelope), and it made sense. It's all one big continuous circle, our confusion, our doubt, our knowing, our pain, our loss, our gain. Flowers rot, make soil, birth more flowers. Same circle.

Death

Later in life, when it did become my grandmother who was "bwoke," and my uncle died of HIV, then passed my stepfather, my aunt, my grandfather, and my soul mate cat, yet I still knew it all as perfect.

Now, the color of death has for me taken on the brownish hue of addiction. Friends have jumped on the third rail in New York, high as a kite after relapsing at ninety days clean and sober. The clients at the rehab where I worked have been rushed off in ambulances with cirrhosis, edema, organ failure, pneumonia, or just wilting like a flower barely clinging to the vine.

My own family has kissed the tongue of the serpent Death, miraculously surviving drunk driving accidents, grand mal seizures from Xanax withdrawal and a cousin's relapses that just wouldn't stop. My own drunken debacles have left me in situations where living was a miracle, and in states of mind where dying would have been a welcome relief.

The Centers for Disease Control says approximately ninety thousand Americans a year die from alcohol-related causes; forty thousand people died in 2015 from drug overdoses, bringing it into the number one slot as the cause of accidental death. Opiate-related death has quadrupled in a decade and a half.

How easy it was for me to understand that after working at a place where people are prescribed card after card of blister packs of punch-out pills to help them level out their withdrawal and manage their conditions. The list is long, including Trazodone, Seroquel, Neurontin, Baclofen,

Topamax, Ativan, Librium, Sinemet, Clonidine, Inderal, Phenergan, Flexeril, Lexapro, and Klonopin. Klonopin, I hate that drug. One of my best childhood friends who's an alcoholic, has taken it for over twenty years to prevent panic attacks, which began as memories of her father molesting her surfaced. I'm told benzodiazepines activate the exact same neurotransmitters in the brain as alcohol. She and I dressed as princesses together when we were eight. And now she almost died in ICU after breaking her leg in three places while drunk dancing. She blew up her friend's apartment in the city, admits to planning her suicide, and having uncontrollable bulimia.

I remember living in LA, at age 28, when I was surrounded by drug culture by way of my lesbian, Nicaraguan, druggie roommate Fran, who sheltered me from the crazier aspects of her life whilst allowing me a little peek into others. She wouldn't allow me to go to certain parties, where she would binge for three days and come back ragged after having shot up horse tranquilizers, meth and coke and called it a "speed-ball", but she introduced me to ecstasy and taught me proper light drug etiquette.

One day she had two drug-dealing friends and neighbors over, and we were discussing the aftereffects of drug and alcohol use, the hangover, the come down, really the withdrawal. Their perspective on the matter was, "If you forget (referring to the bad feelings), do more drugs!"

My theory was that when you do drugs and drink a lot, it is like taking out a second mortgage on your joy. The aftereffects of drunken and high debauchery are a soul-deep bankruptcy which is often referred to in recovery as our

Death

"God-sized hole." In other words, where we long to see Jesus's face in the plywood walls, we instead look for it in our drugs of choice and, in effect, dig that yearning-hole deeper.

If you accept one end of the circle, you accept it all, for there is no end.

I remember being surrounded by tools of incipient sobriety at The Pavillon, a rehab where I worked recently, trying to discover my new sober calling. There were books like Commitment to Sobriety, Codependent No More, Drinking: A Love Story, and words on the counselor's doors: Anne Frank's, "Whoever is happy will make others happy too," and "Life is a gift." Sartre's, "We are our choices," Gandhi's top ten words of wisdom, the St. Francis Prayer and my favorite, a lemur looking tense in a meditative pose with the caption, "Come on inner peace! I don't have all day."

I once asked my favorite patient at the rehab, Marty, what he thought of death. He's a Yale-graduated Episcopalian gay priest who is always carrying around Jung's Man and His Symbols and has been twice defrocked for his drug and alcohol abuse and related shenanigans. He said he thinks that the idea of the circle is good in theory, but overall, fear prevails. He says he would like to embrace the beauty of the circle, but he is overwhelmed by the fear of what comes next. "After all, I'm a rich white man; nowhere for me to go but down."

And in his saying that, I realize what he is lacking, what we all lack when we can't evade the grips of addiction, destructive behavior, fog, depression, shame. It's Faith. With a capital F, for if we fear the unknown, we are truly lacking the belief of what lies beneath, the Universe's great big unending perfect circle.

Dylan Thomas, who died of alcoholism, regaled the fight against death in his plea, "Do not go gentle into that good night." But he also admits, "Wise men, at their end, know dark is right." [1]

I choose not to fight. Anymore. That is step one, total surrender. The acceptance that I have been beaten down. That my way does not work and that, in some ways my will has to be dead so I can avoid the other kind of death. I no longer want to rage or wage war against anything, create drunken drama. No. I accept it; I accept all of it.

THE LIGHT: MY MOM

Dusty, dark attic bedroom, mosquitoes as giant as grapefruits, fans blazing, only making hot air move faster, the only normally soothing sound in the room is the rhythmical squeak of a rocking chair, now monument still. Suddenly, she has swooped me up and away, my sweaty little form paralyzed by the Southern August heat. After minutes in the car, we are at her boss's house, in a guest room. There is A/C. I don't remember ever sleeping better.

Such a world of divide between where I was in our creaky wooden house on Davie Circle with seven renters and twelve cats, legs spangled and welts like sand dollars from those big bug bites, to this designer bedroom set, cool air, nice comforter. Necessary relief. I can still see that bedroom in my mind's eye and love it.

Mom may have sometimes struggled too much, not had enough time or been afraid of contaminating me with whichever form of her not-enough-ism she was currently ruminating over or experiencing, but when it mattered, she always made things right. Like the time she was taking me home in the middle of the night when I was almost too young to retain the memory. But this night is etched indelibly on my just-forming consciousness; we are almost rolling down a hill, rocks and mud and rain roiling beneath her feet. I look down; white heels cling mercilessly to what appears to be a sliding river bank. There is rain everywhere like a breathing ocean, surrounding us, pounding my little arms, which were sleeping just seconds ago but now are wrapped around her neck, hands knotted in her hair, pulling it out from her nurse's cap. What is going on? Hard to tell. She had just gotten off a late shift and picked me up to go home in a raging storm, down the steep muddy hill across the swinging bridge that leads there.

The earth felt unstable and perhaps, because of this moment, that feeling will always resurface. But one thing is clear, she navigated the tumult with grit and surety and we were always going to be alright.

As I got older, I sometimes felt embarrassed by her audacity, her unwillingness to fit into any mold (although there were none that would hold us) and her forthright charge to get what we needed by any means necessary. I remember the alarm clock incident like it were yesterday, a time during which the seed was planted that someday I would be proud to live in that kind of audacity.

We are in JCPenney I have finally gotten a clock radio that I have been wanting forever and it doesn't work. We are given rude treatment by the staff, told that they have no more of that item in stock and that their store policy is to make an exchange only for the exact same item, which they don't happen to have, so oh well. Somehow it seems their lackadaisical attitude is partially enhanced by the absence of a father figure.

The Light: My Mom

My mom makes a scene. I am mortified. This has been common during my eleven long years, moments of sheer embarrassment as it seems my mother has to be outrageous in so many ways, on so many levels, just to get us by.

I am hiding in the aisles by the door to the manager's office. For some reason, in those days the store had a small pharmacy section, so I am peering out from behind rows of yellow Listerine and Johnson & Johnson dental floss. A crowd has gathered. A lower management staffer is corroborating the statement made by the salesperson, stating that their refund policy is very strict.

All I can surmise from the exchanges is that they are not able to do anything because they do not have another matching clock radio in-house. To me, this seems reasonable. The acceptance that I have been dealt a bum hand is as natural as grass is green. All I want in the world is to flee, to get out of this situation where now the whole world knows it.

"I am not leaving from this spot until I speak to your supervisor!"

"Ma'am, I'm sure my supervisor will tell you the exact same thing because it is our store policy and we are very strict on it."

"That doesn't mean that it is right or that I am going to accept it! My little girl saved her hard earned allowance for months to come to your store and purchase this particular clock radio which, after just ten days, has ceased working, and you basically want me just to tell her, 'Oh well, you win some you lose some,' when it is your store's fault for selling her faulty merchandise?! You think she'll understand that?"

I am standing eight feet away, behind the Listerine, and I'm thinking, "Yeah Mom, I understand. It's okay. Can we please just go?"

The crowd has grown; there must be twenty to thirty people watching the battle between the single working mom and the big, bad retail store men. She stands tall, nearly six feet in her brown, heeled boots, her black hair permed and full like a gypsy, her body ensconced in this camel-wool cape coat which gives her the appearance of having wings. I am trembling. Now the world knows we are freaks.

"Did someone call for a supervisor?" Out walks a large, black man in a very official-looking shiny gray suit to confront the mob. He immediately assesses the situation with a nod while my mother explains our dilemma for the third time. He is quiet and resigned. He simply says, "Wait here; let me go see something."

He goes into the secret back bowels of the store and emerges after what seems like twenty minutes. I am so nervous I almost pee my pants. He is carrying a box. What is that? Could it actually be? No. Perhaps just a box. For me?

"As my assistant manager stated, we do not have the model your daughter selected from our store, and our

The Light: My Mom

usual policy is very strict when it comes to exchanges. But I am going to make an exception in your case and give you the next, more expensive model of clock radio. Will that be a suitable solution for you, ma'am?"

I am aghast. No way. It's not possible. I may actually come out of this horrible scene, in which I was resigned to accept the fact that I obviously don't deserve the clock radio I had been dreaming about for months on end because something secret down deep inside of me is unworthy, with a brand new, bigger, better one? It seems like a dream.

Suddenly I am not ashamed of my mom. Suddenly I feel like we belong in the world. Just then, she turns right toward me where I thought I was hidden in the aisle and asks, "Ali?" I nod.

The manager is relieved, anxiously anticipating our eminent departure. She grabs the box, turns on her heel, and walks triumphantly to where I cower. There is applause. I reach out and grab and join her as we careen victoriously toward the door. Grasping her hand, I whisper, "Way to go, Mom."

From all these accrued moments, I learned that life will be hard. We seem to be some kind of exception to all the rules in our single-working-mom and lonely-only child, semi-hippie state. There will be chaos, unfairness and difficulty, but we have to stick together. This is a strong woman. I could learn a lot from her.

Mom and the Fair

We always went to the state fair. No matter what, she made priorities for necessary fun in childhood, but not always in the highest of style. It had always been apparent that having wealth and achievement put certain other families onto a different level, which seemed to trump mine. Being two females, a single working mother and a lonely only child, on our own with seemingly insurmountable daily struggles, that golden carrot of freedom and choice seemed miles away.

I looked at the ideal of the proverbial Jones' and had come out feeling like a loser, poor, disheveled, and less-than in many ways. The Jones' lives seemed to be filled with some kind of secret elixir, their normalcy and ample double income salves against disease, formula for a perfect family, magic.

I remember once when Mom was driving me to school, she had been divulging deep secrets of our inoperable budget and suddenly burst into tears, screaming, "Life is soooo hard!!!!!" She beat the steering wheel and snot flowed freely as I trembled with shock in the passenger seat, but even more notably, with remembrance of what I would always carry with me of what life really was, what work was, and how earning money seemed crucial and elusive. She was burned-out and we seemed to be just barely scraping by, but at what cost? She was running a psychiatric ward at Durham County General Hospital, working too hard, being scolded by her male superiors for arriving late to staff meetings because of dropping me off at school and for the other ways she couldn't perform like a man could.

We weren't poor, but we cut corners where we could, and time. My hair was always scraggly and my clothes second-hand. I remember the shame of wrong sizes, a winter coat covering my hands because it had to be able to last three years, a dress way too small because I loved it and wanted to wear it for as long as I could.

Never was our lack more clear than the year I was eleven and we went to the fair. I loved the fair, the sheer celebration of it, like a party for fall, fortified by the smells of candy apples, sizzling sausages, pigs and hay; the dirt clouded up by pounding, excited feet as they trampled on to the next ride; my feet as they scurried to join the joy.

That year, however, she told me there had to be a plan because money was particularly tight. She asked me if I wanted to ride rides or play games. She'd gone on a date once and had apparently gone to the state fair, because I'd woken up with a bright blue teddy bear in my bed, the kind with the beanbag balls inside, and I had decided that to win those prizes meant to belong. I wanted those prizes. All the teenage girls with boyfriends who piggy-backed life sized pandas all night–that was love. The kids whose daddies had three or four different fluffy, colorful toys draped over their various limbs and busting out of their pockets, they must manage to do everything right and with ease.

I don't know how she knew of my longing because I never shared things like that with her, but her desperation to persevere proved that she did; and I didn't want her to feel bad. Maybe it was her own longing or the obvious gimmick of the fair baiting us all invariably with desire for success, for attaining, for obtaining the prize!

We decided to spend the night devoted to it, to ride only one ride and play a few games. I don't remember the ride, but I do remember the failure. All the hope that went into each basketball throw, the pressure squeezed into each ping-pong toss, fake gunshot, dart throw and baseball hurl until I prickled with the discomfort of not being able to help her win.

We were sad as we ate our polish sausages that night, distracted by thoughts of upcoming possibilities, plans for eschewing this entrenching doom. We forewent the fried dough in favor of another shot, two more games. It seemed three dollars was a lot for those types of crap shoots, especially since they always got you hooked when they declared, "Ohhhh soooo close, just one away," and asked for just one more dollar for one more try, and then another and another and, "Oh! So close! The lady loses again! Better luck next time!"

It was the end of the night and our fair money had been depleted long ago. We had dipped into the grocery cash three games ago and for the third time, Mom said, "Okay, Ali, last try. After this, we go home."

It was like the movies as the tension rested on the arc of that ping-pong ball flying carelessly through the air and then, hallelujah, somehow, miraculously landing in that tiny fish bowl! Finally. The weight lifted from my chest. The smallest prizes were offered, but a prize nonetheless. The gamekeeper motioned Vanna White-style toward the front row of miniscule-looking trinkets, and then explained how we could forego said not-yet-even-chosen accolade, for one more shot at the slightly bigger prizes, tiny teddy bears. And then those could be denied for yet another shot at the next size up, which if won, would offer a shot at the bigger, then the bigger, then the bigger, then the HUGE, life-sized red teddy bear which loomed over our heads like the Cadillac of all fair prizes.

As Mom hesitated and looked like she was thinking about it; I scanned that front row quickly and forcefully said, "That one! I'll take that!" pointing at a little silver tomahawk pendant with a turquoise in the back of the blade. I spent the whole walk back to the car telling Mom how much I loved it and how proud I was of her; after all, it was a Native American-like thing and that was the blood we were the most proud of in our veins.

After two weeks, the head of the faux silver tomahawk broke away from its handle. But I kept that head and treasured it always. Turns out, as I've grown up, I realize how stupid those gigantic stuffed animals are. So atrociously excessive and ridiculous, much like all the other prizes and achievements our culture seems to blindly convince us we are in dire need of.

I learned how to tuck money away, to hide it from myself in ways that would make it last and be ready for me when I needed it. I learned to give myself many little treats, and learned how make enough of it to feel not so straggly and second hand, and to always be able to afford fried dough at the fair! But most importantly, I learned to never, ever underestimate the value of the love you cannot prove with a prize.

Caterpillar
Or, Who I want to Be

When I was five years old, I found a caterpillar in a mud puddle at Victory Village, my preschool. I carefully picked up its soggy, tubular form, acutely aware of how squishy it was, my two fingers almost touching through its middle. I gently dabbed its fur with my dress, soaking up as much of the water as possible; it seemed soaked through. I held it between my two hands and breathed warm air into a gap between my fingers, hoping to dry it.

As the end of recess drew near, I took it to my cubby, the little wooden cubicle where we put our tiny people's collection of important things—a lunchbox and a thermos, little projects like red construction paper with glue and glitter. I laid it gently on my cubby's soft pine floor and closed the door. I checked it between classes, which at that stage were more like micro-events, play practice for our great American preschool play, Stone Soup (I was a carrot), nap time, and making no-bake chocolate, peanut butter, and oatmeal cookies. I would adjust the caterpillar's body to ensure it was drying evenly, not entirely sure it wasn't dead. This was a day-long exercise and one which consumed my entire consciousness.

At the end of the school day, I took out the little fuzzy caterpillar and held it in my tiny, cupped hand, and brought it up to my eye for inspection. At first it was still, but the fact that it was staying upright on its little black rubbery feet—unlike when it was initially rescued from its watery doom flopping here and there indiscriminately—was encouraging. Then, as if it woke out of a coma, it began crawling along quickly, tippety tappety on my hand as if nothing had ever happened. It wandered up my arm and I put my other hand to my shoulder for continued, watch-able perambulation. It traversed my right palm, then on down into the white playground sand and off to a nearby tree where I imagined it reunited with its family.

That was one of the most satisfying experiences of my life and one that I always carry with me as a quintessential reflection of my own soul. My idea of a life worth living became clearer in the world. One lesson, to give anything you have in reserve to another being in a time of need; no, beyond that. Truly loving and respecting the other versions of life around us was paramount. There was an awe in the face of nature, which in turn assured an irrefutable and humbling awareness that some great, brilliant superpower existed and was in charge of such perfection.

As I grew older, staying true to that wise little girl, I stated every year for my New Year's resolution, "I want to be the me I want to be." In time, I woke up to the brutal reality that living up to that resolution is more difficult than it sounds. The chasm between who I was in that little pocket of light, deep down inside, and who I was every day, was growing wider.

For example, I didn't want to be that girl who, desperate in her heartbreak at feeling she was losing her soul mate to whom she'd promised forever—and meant it at seventeen—was now calling him on the phone after having guzzled three quarters of a bottle of red wine, Mom's loaded .38 Special in her hand, threatening to blow her head off if he didn't come over. No, I never dreamt up that version of Snow White's ending when I fantasized, in a post-Disney high or lying in a field, how sweet it would be for the one I loved to simply touch my chin with his fingers.

I also did not dream of the day I passed out on the Q train traveling between 57th Street and Coney Island, traveling back and forth twice all the way after a solo New York City drinking binge. Even in sobriety I behave badly, receiving proof of the continuous work that must be done. No matter how much therapy I complete through healing sessions, prayers, meditations and journeys of seeking, as I age, I accrue this sludgy layer of goop that makes it more and more challenging to communicate the wishes of that deeply treasured and enlightened little girl I started out as. I guess that's part of the human experience.

But we have to try. After leaving what had been my home – the home Nanda and I had moved into after marriage in 2014 (a shack, really with a landlady who did not believe in locks) because it was suddenly unbearable, my car lodged, slanting in a snowy ditch where I had tried and failed to get to work after an onslaught of wintry mix weather. My heart pounding, hands shaking, feeling unsafe and crazy, I called a neighbor whom I barely knew to rescue me. She had given me a massage in exchange for Indian cooking lessons and a jar of chai. She, her fiancé, and their new roommate took me in, soothed me. They offered me their food, shoulders, computer, and couch.

I have now filled my belly with chicken chili, emptied my woeful bladder and sipped much needed water. In this moment, I experienced heaven on earth. Sartre says, "Hell is other people," but that means that, inversely, the opposite can also be true. That is true in recovery, for without the help of other alcoholics, I could never get well. I guess it's because we need constant reminding. There is sometimes an insurmountable tendency towards feeling alone.

It took this miserable February weather and some life-saving neighbors to remind me that those things I held true as a five-year-old rescuing the caterpillar are always well within our reach.

REASON, SEASON OR LIFETIME

I tried my best over the years to maintain the ideals of that little caterpillar-saver, but as my alcoholism developed, I went wrong at many turns. I chose to go to my hometown college, the University of North Carolina, Chapel Hill (UNC). It was a success, but it could have been better.

I graduated on time with a double major in English and Dramatic Arts, having entered as a writer and exited as an actor/movie star wanna-be. I worked in restaurants after to save money for movie star school, The American Academy of Dramatic Arts. My favorite restaurant was Fearrington House, a five diamond Relais and Chateaux in Pittsboro, N.C.

I fell in love with a tremendous man named Joris (whom I should've married) and worked to save money for the move to LA LA land and then worked to get out of a DWI but finally made it. Los Angeles was an exciting lesson in learning to act and practicing art. I did make it through three years of the school, proudly making it into the third year repertory company as the number one woman on the "B list", one of only sixteen out of the initial two thousand applicants. I did well but could have done better. Then, right before 9/11, at thirty years old I moved to New York, the final step in exploring my wild, party side which eventually brought me to sobriety, thank God. But I couldn't have done it without Eddie.

Reality is relative. At the time when he said, "People come into your life for a reason, a season or a lifetime," I thought we had a lifetime awaiting us. I desperately wanted to reassure him--that little Eddie I saw in his bright, wide, long-lashed, gaping brown eyes who'd been abused by his Puerto Rican father, off his rocker, off his meds, who'd nearly killed him for skipping his only class ever--as he asked me if I'd promise him I'd never leave. But, as one of his other mantras affirmed, "Life has no guarantees."

I first met Eduardo Sepulveda when I was a new general manager of Merchants NY Café in downtown Manhattan, and probably in a little over my head. He was the concierge of 90W, the luxury apartment building that housed my restaurant.

"Ali, iss Eddie," said Johnny, the busser who had answered the phone, which in my opinion, had no business ringing in the middle of lunch.

"Yeah, yeah, tell him I know!"

Two minutes later, the same persistent ring interrupted my reverie of guest serving, swooshing around trying to compensate for some oversight or understaffing on my part, because I loved to fix everything.

"He says is really bad this time." Johnny pleaded in his lilted Mexican trill for me to remove this awkward hassle from his already overloaded plate. He also seemed sympathetic for Eddie.

"Okay, okay!!" I replied as I grabbed the can of mango deodorizer spray (but not just any deodorizer spray–this was Time Mist 9000, the highly concentrated odor counteractant, chemically engineered to attack and neutralize unpleasant smells, like exhaust grease particles as revealed to me by my mentor, Richard Starwalt, my Obi-Wan) and flew toward the door. I ran out into the freezing cold Manhattan fall, flying from my door to his, ten feet away, into his perfectly polished marble and steel lobby, straight to the right where there was a huge wall-sized vent panel, and began vigorously shaking and spraying the aerosol can's nozzle up into the louvers of the bottom panel.

"Uh, yeah, so, it's really bad, Ali. I don't know; something's gotta change. I got tenants complaining left and right. My whole lobby smells like hamburgers, which, if it were up to me would be great, but you gotta remember we got some very rich vegetarians up in this here super-luxury joint!"

"I know! I know!" I said, as I rushed right behind him, behind the front desk to spray into the other intake vent. "I've got it all under control and I'm sorry!" I apologized as I ran around the back wall to the mailbox area to catch the secretly stashed extra vent which I just knew had vast circulation value, and tackled it with my miracle mango spray.

"Look," I shouted through the twenty foot-high-ceilinged, echoing elevator area, "I have the guy coming Tuesday, I told you!"

"Ali, it's Thursday; you've been saying that for a week."

"Oh, is it Thursday already? Huh! Well, I'll call him again today, but I gotta get back to lunch, okay?!"

"But," he beseechingly blurted as I bolted out his front door to casually careen back through mine.

Ring. Ring. Ring. Oh my God, the phone again? "Merchants NY Café, this is Ali, how may I help you?"

"Yo, Ali, it's Eddie. I don't know if you noticed, but I don't think we finished our conversation. So, like I was sayin', you said the guy would be here two days ago, so, like, whadda you think is up with that?" His South Bronx accent was cute and pushy all at once.

"I told you, I'll call him today and get him here as soon as possible. It looks like we have to install an electrostatic precipitator and that's not an instant fix, so in the meantime, if I just stay more on top of the spraying and do it before it accumulates we should be okay, yes?"

"Okay, Ali, okay, okay. Sounds good. Thank you. Let me know when he comes, okay?"

"Okay. Talk to you later, bye." I hung up and rolled my eyes, thinking this guy was just a little over-involved for a glorified doorman.

Turns out he thought I was a little crazy, buzzing around like a feeble fly, trying to put out a fire with a tissue.

But we were kindred spirits, destined to touch each other's lives irrevocably. He was a workaholic and so was I. He was his boss's right-hand man, and so was I. We were both taken out of the trenches of hard menial labor, he from doorman/handyman to superintendent, me from server to general manager/owner-in-spirit of this classy, busy New York restaurant.

Who knew that simply having what I considered normal work ethic (well, my great grandma showed up at her own wedding with her hands in binds from working the farm at five am right before, that's normal, right?) would merit me such respect from my boss, Abraham Merchant. Somehow he picked me out of the pool of no-show actors and models to lure into management from the get go and eventually "give me" my own restaurant (his words) to run, Merchants NY Café, in the heart of the Financial district of Manhattan, in the wake of 9/11. We had both been elevated to positions of the highest responsibility in our mutual establishments because we were good people; our bosses knew they could rely on, exploit, and demand excellence from us.

We spent every waking moment in that building. He put in door sweeps to keep out the cold winter, replaced handles and taught my entire staff the neglected art of proper Windexing—did you know you have to wash the glass first? Then you use the sponge side of the squeegee to get a glass so clear a bird could fly through it; in fact one time, a drunken guest did walk through a glass door and developed a contusion the size of a grapefruit.

Eddie spent six hours one afternoon dissecting my stand-up heater to try and replace its thermocouple; I think it took taking it apart and reassembling it five times before it emitted heat once again.

We became best friends. I gave his tenants a ten percent discount and his staff fifty, and made a point of treating them all as VIPs. He spoiled me with free HVAC filters, patio pressure washing, Windex and Fantastik. Granted, his boss was an Investor, so the relationship was encouraged and felt professionally beneficial. He spent hours with another handyman one day trying to fix my fifteen-ton A/C unit on my triple whammy day; on my birthday, the exhaust, the A/C, and the air intake that keeps the whole cooling system balanced and flowing, they all crashed. I could also sleep in his apartment just above the restaurant and become even more consumed than I already was in the restaurant life. Once, I went to the basement to personally check in a Sysco truck food order in my pajamas.

Eddie and I fell in love over Tom Cat Bakery's semolina rolls with sesame seeds and coffee. We could talk shop and managerial stresses and rewards for days on end. It was a glorious thing, professionally. But personally, our relationship was a disaster, encouraged in its insanity by a constant flow of booze: Bacardi and cokes, and later, Sauvignon blanc. Our eventual engagement and then cohabitation was a gauntlet we ran for three long years of our five year entanglement, trapped in the mutual respect on which we founded our bond and the deep love which had concretized it. It was a sticky-tar, molasses muck of verbal and emotional abuse, anguish and torment. Pure hell.

But in the end, I wouldn't trade anything for it. After living together for two years and sometimes not speaking for days, Eddie looked at me and simply said, as my friend, the man whom I trusted with my life and career, "Ali, I think you got a drinking problem." I fought it with all my heart and soul, until our sheets, stained with red wine vomit, blotted out my denial so that I woke up one day and knew he was right.

The typhoon of my alcohol abuse had finally reached its messy but necessary bottom. Without him, I may have taken too long to come into the rooms of recovery. Without him, I never would've survived the biggest professional challenge and accomplishment of my life. Without him, I may not have gone to India. Without him, I may not have come to know Buddha, having watched endless films on the Siddhartha story. Without him, I may not have gotten to visit Buddha's birthplace in Lumbini, Nepal or seen the Bodhi tree under which Buddha woke up in Bodhgaya, the Dalai Lama's home.

I sent Eddie a leaf from that Bodhi tree and a prayer scarf which I got blessed by the Dalai Lama. I called him for closure upon their sending. I kept a blog on Google called "Life Re-Boot", recounting my life in recovery and my tumultuous life-rearrangement, beginning with the fulfillment of a dream by going to India where I volunteered at Ramana's Garden, home for destitute children. He said he'd read it, every word and enjoyed watching some enlightenment there.

I think of him almost every day. I pray that that little boy who was almost killed by his own father's foot at his throat has continued on his healing path, with Buddha, Joseph Campbell, and Jung. We've spoken since and it is good to know that he is well, living in Texas, has learned to drive, and is successfully remodeling a luxury lake house. I credit him for my salvation because I know that without his partnership, I could very well be dead, permanently drunk, or at the very least, still miserable and broken, and for that I am eternally grateful.

Sobriety and Kindness: My Bottom

It was night time and I was at the bar, again. His name was Tony and he had promised me cigarettes.

It all started gloriously enough, my usual respite from a night of stressful, busy zooming around the restaurant, helping to serve, directing staff, and tending to the guests in a way that made each and every one of them feel like a VIP. The respite seemed deserved and harmless–a glass of red wine at BLT, the upscale bar inside the W hotel, where I felt like the classy clientele, simply unwinding after a hard day's work; a glass of wine and perhaps a few appetizers to call dinner?

I never ate while I was serving guests. I was a bit old school from my experience at the Fearrington House which was a Five Diamond Relais & Châteaux (a global fellowship of luxury hotels and restaurants). I also learned to never lean, never touch my hair or my face, and to never eat in front of guests. In fact, we had not been able to leave the floor for hours, bathroom use prohibited for the entirety of an eight-hour dinner shift–a phenomenon which caused me to have what I referred to as waitress bladder, the pain of urgency dissipating into a tingle of nothing for endless hours, only to resurface when relief was in store, a talent I prided myself on. So I had to go for some dinner.

The only thing was that this classy dinner ritual often included many unnamed and free refills by the various bartenders who knew me and knew I too suffered in those thresholds of hell we call the restaurant business, having been in the trenches to rise to the glorious top where I was Ali Webster, General Manager, with business cards to prove it. We call this stealthy, graceful flowing of the booze, our "industry discount" and I loved it. And often the pouring of various wines, new ones which they thought I'd appreciate and therefore had to sample, often preponderated the dinner part, as I would forget to order anything as the kitchen silently fell into closed.

This night seemed like one of those classy escapades like any other. But when I say "any other" I have to mention that one such night led to a taxi ride home which I recorded with my Blackberry, and would keep as a reminder for a year and eight months into sobriety until it was stolen in Nepal, to remind me of what a mess of not-myself I was under the influence of alcohol, slurring and babbling incoherently, but believing I was solving the driver's marital problems. A reminder that try as I might, once I started consuming alcohol, I could never seem to stop.

Tony was just another married businessman staying at the hotel, seemingly in search of some likewise respite from his tired and untrue life and an opportunity to be untrue to his wife. The thing is that I vowed to never be that woman. The idea of being on the other end of betrayal in the form of adultery disgusted me. I also had never cheated on my fiancé, Eddie, no matter how many times we had broken up, his verbal and emotional abuse keeping me in a prison of confusion, unable to move toward or away from him. He had taken the diamond ring back, or I had proffered it many times, twelve I counted. But I had at least remained loyal to him and our relationship in that way, vowing not to be the cheater I had been in my twenties, especially since this was the man I wanted to commit my life to, and if I could just do that better than my parents, perhaps my life would work.

Tony bought me drinks and I threw them back. I usually had to have a cigarette after one or two; the craving for a habit I absolutely deplored was also a tell-tale signal that I was severely out of whack, the proof being in the pudding of my nightly twelve-dollar-a-pack purchase which I would then promptly discard on the way home, vowing tomorrow would be different. I would also change it up, Parliament Lights, then Marlboro Mediums, maybe throw in Lucky Strikes to send my system into a tailspin of knowing it did not have that addiction. Sadly, at this point in the evening, I had no cigarettes. Tony vowed getting me cigarettes to be his quest as if he were my knight in shining armor rescuing me from some gloom; only he was no knight.

We went to the next bar where Amy worked. She used to work at many different restaurants within my company, but had finally been fired after years of severe alcoholism, passing out at company functions and finally, stealing money she was owed from a guest check, saying they hadn't paid. She had resigned to this quiet little corner of the world, near Wall Street in the dive bar where serious drinkers often finished up the night, and where I always got free shots and never remembered anything after them.

After that same repeated embarrassing block in memory, I woke up in a hotel room with Tony on his bed. He was trying to undress me and I was fighting hard against semi-consciousness. I remember him grabbing and painfully sucking on my breasts, pain which would leave bruises that would stay around for two weeks–into Christmas. I remember intercourse, safe, but unwanted, a blur of limbs and his strange face and vomit. It was one of the scariest moments of my life. But it was also definitive evidence that I could no longer believe I had any control over alcohol, and that when imbibing, I had no control over any aspect of my life, including my own body. It may have been heartbreaking, but that simple admission saved my ass because who knows what the next "Tony" might have done.

Looking back, I can only regard that Ali with the utmost compassion. Addiction is prevalent and my heart is full for all those who are finding their way on that path. After Eddie had first helped shine the light on my obvious problem I had continued to spiral down for another few months. I would try to stop n my own, only ever making it about two weeks at the most, every time the first night would be a shaky, sweaty, sleepless night of what I now know as withdrawal. You would think coming out of that would be enough to warrant not going back to needing it, but it wasn't. Once I started I couldn't stop. It was like,

Sobriety and Kindness: My Bottom

once the decision had been made to pick up that first drink, the ceaseless locomotive of want had been fully fueled and placed in throttle ahead, so that I was trapped in a prison of continuation.

It took me weeks of tribulations before I could surrender. There were nights of pure hell, red wine vomit on tangled ripped down shower curtain, drinking until 3:00 a.m. at a dive bar near my house while the world hunkered down for the Blizzard of 2011 in New York City, so that by the time I stumbled home, the snow was up to my knees and whirling around me in a flurry. A little old lady I believed to be a neighbor seemed to be having trouble getting to her apartment, but when I offered her my help, she simply looked at me, gazed at my weaving and bobbing form disguised in a fancy wool overcoat, shirt untucked from dry-cleaned trousers, cigarette dangling half smoked from dry lips, bleary eyes caked and squinting against the furious wind, and said, "No, thank you" firmly enough to make an impression.

I also experienced another night during which, in a final attempt to save the relationship with Eddie, I decided that I would clean the canopy bed panels. They were a coarse muslin fabric and had been chosen expressly as the appropriate addition to this, my soul mate bed, for their natural simplicity and basic goodness.

But his incessant incense burning seemed to aggravate my allergies, which in turn aggravated his irascibility, since I coughed and complained, which caused him to yell and taunt and tell me how screwed up I was for being so weak. Suddenly, at 1:30 a.m., I decided I had the cure for my allergic reaction and his response. It wasn't the incense; it was the panels. They had never been washed and were probably dusty and the doctor said it was dust, not incense I was allergic to, so here I could just pluck them off like ripe fruit and throw them in the wash and voilà! Instant wedding and happily ever after!

But alas, the panels were looped over the bed frame in such a way that each post had to be unscrewed to slide them off their bars, the unscrewing of which caused the whole square top to topple down onto the bed, where I joined it, in disarray, to sleep in the muck with my fancy long-tailed beige suit, a sight Eddie had to crawl over to go off to work, as it also blocked the doorway.

I finally surrendered. I asked Nancy my therapist to help me and she left me a voicemail with two possibilities for a meeting. I wanted something away from home and away from work, that landed me at a clubhouse in Times Square. I limped up pastel pink and green stairs, in a cloud of urine smell and emerged into relief and Abby, who was miraculously speaking my story.

My first night without alcohol, I trembled with fear, angst and sweat; decades of shoved-underground emotions and shadows were unearthing themselves along with all the toxins that gladly freed themselves from my cells. And then I called her–Abby, my new soon-to-be sponsor in recovery, at 3:45 a.m. And she helped me. I had never even cried out to my own mother from any discomfort in all my growing-up life, in fact, it had been her that had done that to me. Someone being there for me saved my life and the memory of it brings tears to my eyes to this day.

The second night, I did the same and she told me to grab hold of my pillow, fluff it up, and shake out all the bad energy and flip it over. Works every time. She would then go on to text me every day, "Happy Day 2!" or "28" or whichever it was, painfully slow until I hit "90," the big landmark in New York, when I had to tell my story in front of the room, to show how important I was. Just kidding.

Abby escorted me lovingly along a path I never could have even gone a step on alone, coaxing me, a year later, out of the relationship with Eddie, holding my hand through constant texting, providing a sense of prevalent permanent support, easing me into continuing sobriety. She met me every Saturday at Pigalle, a French Bistro on Eighth Ave. guided me through the steps, made me raise my hand to sponsor after a year until I had three sponsees! Supported me as I decided to leave New York after eighteen months of this walk.

She is one of the most important people in my life and the kind of debt you feel owed toward an angel of that magnitude almost defies words, and all that is ever required is to pay it forward. But suffice it to say, I love you, Abby; without you I might not be.

This paying it forward in the program is part of the service which sets us free. There is a painting that I love called, The Man on the Bed, featuring three alcoholics. It represents to me the first-ever meeting. In the picture there is a detoxing alcoholic; he wears a white wifebeater and sits slumped in a yellow dingy light on a rickety bed. Bill W. and Dr. Bob face him, in suits, armed with papers, leaning in with alacrity. It captures so perfectly one alcoholic helping another, from a place of understanding, of having been there, with no moral high ground, preaching or judgment. That this and only this can help save another sufferer. This was a medicine that eluded even the illustrious Dr. Jung who declared that man in the wifebeater was "hopeless". He later met this man sober and he hardly recognized him; he was amazed that this medicine had succeeded where he himself had failed.

The spiritual experience of working with others who come from a common place has been proven to be the key to changing patterns of selfishness and self-centered destruction. It has helped guide me to my current work as an aide and Med Tech in a retirement community where just last night I was referred to by a co-worker as a "walking trophy of grace," because I have learned to practice some of these principals in my affairs.

I have been blessed to come in contact with those who would help me as well as those who have needed my help. I have come to trust the Divine, whom I usually call "God," and am learning more and more to hand things over to that power rather than rest in my own disastrous ego and will. I am learning to learn, and living to serve. This is nothing short of a miracle.

The Day I Decided to Reboot

It turns out that sobriety is not enough on its own. Apparently there follows an entire overhaul of your whole inner engine; in other words, we are drunks or druggies, gamblers, sexaholics, love addicts, overeaters etc., for a reason.

We learn in the rooms of recovery that it is ourselves that are the problem. We can remove the drink, but if we don't do something about the person that remains lonely and bereft without it, we will invariably go back to it or move on to another addiction. The overhaul. I have found that help in the fourth step (a rigorous and honest attempt to take a thorough inventory of oneself, with the goal being to get rid of unhelpful elements and be better fit to serve), but it has taken a few years to get there.

In my early sobriety, I tortured my staff and my restaurant with my frustration and intensity. But I was doing the best I could at that point. Until I couldn't do it at all anymore.

It had taken much struggle to find a niche where I shone, in the city of my dreams. The restaurant business. I had risen from server to general manager in three years in a whirlwind of New York-minute style chaos, in over my head, loving the power, the glory, the martyrdom-like sweat and tears, and having several emotional breakdowns to show for it. I had arrived.

But it took its toll, along with the undiagnosed alcoholism, and turned this girl scrambled in no time. One of the straws that broke the camel's back was a server of mine named Viktoryia, "Vika" for short. Don't let the cute name fool you, she was Belarusian and worked for me for five years in the café. She had typical Eastern European traits, hardworking, very passionate, extreme in nature, going from a sweet little bird to a hateful, murderous Cruella in seconds.

People were afraid of her, new bussers especially. She terrorized them. She bet me once that she could bus her own tables and do better than if she had any bussers. She did it. Sunday brunch, sixty covers (total guests all shift), all while seven months pregnant.

On the day I realized that this mini-career of mine was coming to an end, she was particularly caustic, exhibiting a passive-aggressive attitude. Every time she passed me, she made jabs about the new busser, Juned, how stupid and incompetent he was. Usually when she behaved this way, for my own sanity, I tried to imagine her as this protective mama bird who felt attacked by outsiders (the Bangladeshi bussers) who took tips from her pocket—worms right out of the mouths of her babies.

But on this day, my hopper was full. I had just managed to escape an emotionally abusive relationship with my ex fiancé after three years of hell; I had been sober for just over a year and was permanently grumpy and wound up tight, too tight to run a restaurant, in fact, I was in a kamikaze, a downward spiral of burnout. Every little bitter comment felt like a caustic knife in my gut, proof that I was a failure, a reason why I had done everything wrong and was a terrible person and pathetic manager.

And then she said them, the words that made me bust: "I shouldn't have to pay him anything because he didn't do anything. He doesn't deserve any of my money!"

I had explained to her countless times how it wasn't her money until she walked out of the restaurant with it and that until then, she just happened to be a cash register, the one responsible the safekeeping of the cash she collected which included the bussers' share of gratuities. Total tip out was lower than most New York City restaurants and, in fact, it is this type of blatant server entitlement and inequity that I believe is making Danny Meyer (NYC's and, as far as I'm concerned, the world's, restaurant God) eliminate tipping altogether. Europe has had it right all these years in abstinence from tipping.

So to hear those words was pure disrespect, hitting me like battery acid, and I blew a gasket. I slammed the cash register door, coins crashing violently inside it, metallic echo amplified in stereo by the tiled wall acoustics. That sweet, European-styled bistro-café which was the only baby I'll ever have, reverberated with my destructive force as I shouted, "With words like that you don't deserve to work here!" And I stormed out of the restaurant into the

Manhattan streets to walk it off, breathe, and try to calm down.

The thoughts came in like the first glimmer of a silvery lining after a storm, my first clarity in a long, long time. I didn't have to do this. I could leave. I needed out. And not just out of the restaurant, or the restaurant business in general, or even out of New York, but out of all of it. Out of my apartment, out of my whole promisingly-successful growing career, out of the city that I loved so much, out of my whole life.

A fog had lifted and I thought, here I was being so sad that I'm forty years old and never managed to get married and have babies, but on the other side of that coin, what did I have? Freedom. I had enough savings to make some choices and I'd always wanted to go to India. I began to tingle with the possibility. The freedom set in like withered roots regenerating for growth. That night I wrote my letter of resignation and emailed it to my boss, who had been like a soul mate boss for twelve years. I called my mom and told her my plans, and I began to research orphanages with which I could volunteer.

This huge life change was finally mine. Up until that point, it felt like my life was lived inside a pinball machine, batted between booze and ego-driven passions such as becoming a movie star or finding Prince Charming. It was like I had been on a speeding locomotive, powered by the pretend freedom of the tornado in the bottle that I couldn't get out of until that moment. I had choices. Ironically, after having quit soon thereafter and taking a year or so off to be with her children, Viktoryia is now working as a manager at one of my former company's sister properties. Karma. The universe puts everything in your path for a reason even when it seems unbearable. I honestly believe that to be true. So, thanks, Vika.

Solo

I'd spent much of my childhood time alone. Some people believe that only children are spoiled, have "lonely child" syndrome, not having had to fight with other siblings over food, parents' gifts, and attention. But I yearned for company, for an older brother to protect me, love me, teach me well. In the absence of that, I came to appreciate the freedom that solitude accorded, an ability to carve out my own little nook in the world so that I could function in it, so that I could flourish, or sometimes wallow.

When I was five, I had a secret hideout in the backyard of our Davie Circle home, underneath the bows of a huge magnolia tree. My stuffed animals accompanied me. We had tea and went hunting. What grand adventures were mine alongside Koala Bear, Kanga and Roo, Raggedy Ann and Andy, and some perpetually hugging monkeys.

Later I would spend hours dancing to Olivia Newton-John, catapulting off the furniture when no one was around. As I became a teen, I learned to journal, authoring an emotional knowledge of myself and the world which would eventually fill ninety-five books. At college's end, my dream turned to acting school in Los Angeles, The American

Academy of Dramatic Arts. I saved money and packed my little world into the gold hatchback Mercury Tracer Mom gave me as a graduation present and set off across the country solo.

The taste of travel was a rich wind in my mouth, lips singing along as the Indigo Girls blared from my radio, cruising through the canyons with red dirt flying by. The damper to this wondrous freedom was totaling my car in the ninth ward of New Orleans, the murder capital of the world, on the corner of Claiborne and Desire. I'd had three beers at lunch, but that couldn't have had anything to do with it.

Finally making it to California in my rented Ford Taurus and purchasing a cheap Nissan automatic, Los Angeles presented a freedom all its own; the wildness, experimenting, and most exciting of all, acting. Learning how to inhabit another life was exhilarating. Researching World War II to become The Girl on the Via Flaminia of Italy who tearfully recalls her brother's guts being blown out in Anzio was a thrill. I can still see it, the older brother I wanted, dead on the white-pebbled shore. I lived vicariously through my characters and enjoyed not being myself.

Later, suffering from an excess of freedom, I once again drove across the country, broke, with my tail between my legs and my cat, Albuquerque in my lap. Believing that L.A. had been my problem instead of admitting to the raging alcoholism I was suffering from, I had scraped myself out of the trenches by my fingernails to move to NY at age 30, in 2001. It was a brave whirlwind as well.

And perhaps a geographic (in recovery this means an attempt to fix the problem by changing your geographic location, as if you didn't take you with you. I think that is why I used to hate that quote, "wherever you go, there you are"). The solo freedom had dissolved into drunkenness, the feeble assertion of a crumbling wild woman who wanted what she wanted when she wanted it and usually took it, for better or worse. Usually worse.

There was nothing as free as giving up alcohol, the biggest adventure of all. Then deciding at eighteen months to give up all my plans; my apartment; my fiancé, Eddie; my career; New York City; my love, Merchants NY Cafe, which was my baby; and the turtles, Latti (short for Latticia) and Bodhi. In my first sober escapade, I flew to India, to explore that magical, wild land on my own, trusting the foreign and spicy earth beneath my feet to swallow me up in a universal hug. Nepal was a surprise on many levels, but more about that later.

Trusting the Universe, the moment brings me joy. I know always that the journey is perfect, even when excruciating.

I went to India (October, 2012) because I expected, in my long eighteen months of sobriety to be ready for a new career and life choice, perhaps becoming the next director of Ramana's Garden. Instead I was demoted in the Organic Café they had there, my ego exposed and flagrantly highlighted as grotesque; apparently the NY restaurateur shtick does not fly at the hip, healthy, spiritual eatery in this yoga capitol of the world where gurus pilgrim and seekers sojourn. I also failed to properly execute my Visa process so it expired after two months and I had to flee to

Nepal for fifteen days to apply for a new one. Then I fell clumsily in love with a lying Nepali man named Nanda Takhari, who was much younger than I. We travelled to Goa on my dime to bask in the sun before returning to his boss (whom he told he'd been to his village back in Nepal to dispute some nasty land disputes). We were then joined by my mom who rafted down the Ganga with us in Nanda's expert hands (he had started as a kayak and trekking guide and had risen to be manager of a local adventure business office).

We had to go down a part of the river where three had drowned in one week. We then travelled alone to Dharamsala, home of the Dalai Lama, and to a Safari in Rajastan, Delhi and the Taj Mahal by way of Mathura, Krishna's birthplace. I then journeyed on alone to Bodghaya (where Siddartha awoke to become Buddha) and back to Rishikesh before flying home.

I returned three months later in July of 2013 to visit my new love's village, Odanaku, in remote Western Nepal because he had made me promise I would while swirling through India's non-traffic ruled streets on the back of his motorcycle. I then returned in January of 2014 to help Nanda obtain his Fiancé Visa and fly home to our wedding in North Carolina.

WHIRLWIND, RAMANA'S GARDEN

Rishikesh, October 2012

It was a seven and a half hour bumpy ride with chickens up the thing I guess they would call a road from Delhi. A young man encroached upon my space with his drunken knee as he grabbed my water bottle to swig from and insisted on needing my thigh for his gangly arms' reach to spread his newspaper.

This was all following a culture earthquake upon arrival in Mumbai. The wrong part. Not the south where they make the movies, but the north where apparently no tourists should go. I figured, "This place knows me; heck, I've had many lifetimes here, right? That's what a psychic had told me. How hard can it be?"

So I had gone alone and booked a random hotel near the airport which nobody, not even the drunks in a half block radius of it, had heard of. The taxi driver had been picking his crusty feet before grabbing my bags to swoop me into his six-decade-looking old car to drive me past sewage smelling, boarded-up midnight streets, and otherwise only darkness to this hidden hotel.

The next day I was unable to find a SIM card to have a working cell phone, change any money, or even get a rickshaw to pick me up. It had all been eye-opening, world-racking chaos until I found a restaurant, went uncharacteristically touristy with the tikka masala, and saved my soul with a Thums Up (Indian coke, with hints of incense and the dustiness of tons of sugar).

None of this was in any way remedied by the quick trip to Rishikesh on that ordinary bus which jostled my guts and my security well beyond a state of coming loose. In my first moment in Ramana's Garden, I gave my future ex-niece my favorite earring from Tibet. Her name is Monica and she was beyond adorable and capable of wresting my prized possessions out of my clutching grip.

Right off the bat I was told I was to take over the organic café, write thirty new menu items, and that I had screwed up on my visa. It expired in a month and a half (I had committed to three months volunteering there and was planning to be in India six). I wait all my life to come here and India is kicking me out.

In desperation, I found a café with a view, Mama Mia. The man running it had a welt the size of a plum on his neck. He tells me it is from a spider, which terrifies me as I see hundreds of spiders in my work in the garden we are cultivating in preparation for the café's opening.

On the path to the garden, I come across another volunteer who has a similar welt and says it is from the furry caterpillars, yellow with long hair and black spots, which also comfortably inhabit the creepy crevices of the food-bearing dirt to which I am destined. Once there, pulling bindi weeds (dead stalks of okra which have expired their season), I began to weep. Ego was cracking. I felt lost, kicked out, stupid, and aimless. The mountains and the dirt barely held my tears.

We have a lunch for twenty-three French Canadians in the café the next evening which is the only time I feel completely comfortable; even though Ankara, the fourteen-year-old manager refuses to listen to any of my suggestions, like how to use seat numbers, write down orders (he uses the raise-your-hands-if-you-want-to-eat-this system), or serve all of one course at a time. We eventually found peace singing The Wizard of Oz and Little Mermaid songs together while dancing Rockette-style and out-hamming each other.

I spent the next day teaching school because a Hindu Festival (of which there are literally hundreds) caused a teacher's absence. I had sixty kids' names to learn and they are so similar and foreign like Durga, Durgi, Burg, Bindi, Bindya, Vindha.

I then was responsible for supervising an after-school study session where they swarmed like deranged monkeys and hit each other beyond my control until finally I said the magic words, "Next time no TV!" Speaking of monkeys, there were many around and they did attack, especially if you had food, so one more responsibility was to protect the kids from death-by-monkey, or more importantly, scare.

The volunteers were needed constantly in the compound, which is both a school for one hundred and sixty and home for sixty-three. I felt held in a taut non-balanced alertness of wanting to help, being useful in a flash, and feeling utterly in the way and uncertain the remainder of the time. Like for example, my first few days in the compound, having been given no rules or guidelines I clumsily asked Sarita about having been kidnapped by a man as I'd been told she had. Apparently he'd taken her into prostitution and she had to be rescued by the director. When a manager had finally arrived I was informed that the inquiry of an unknown volunteer into her past had caused her to be suicidal.

I was told of a python that had just left the kitchen the day before I entered it, having rolled off the top of the windowsill down onto the counter where Chanda (the Nepali woman who would become my soul sister) had been cutting spinach.

When I tried to sleep, there was this loud, angry hissing sound outside my little hut. Gopala, the assistant boss, searched around for it and attempted to soothe me by saying it was only cicadas. The director, Prabhavata Dwabha ("Prabha") suggested it was a peacock, which would have been lovely. The girls said definitively that it was a large frog. When I ask Prabha if it could be a cobra, she says, "Well, yes, there are millions of them around here!" The next day the kids told me they saw one on the beach when they went to do laundry on the Ganga's shore.

Sleepless, itchy (Bedbugs? Chiggers? Baby cobra or fuzzy caterpillar bites?), moldy and dirty—I was barraged by kids that could always use help, love, attention, and care. Oh, and there were scorpions in my room? Prabha said their bites only give one nights' fever, so it's not that big of a deal.

But it seemed worth it all as I told the ten-year-old boys bedtime stories recounting the movies Ghost and Jurassic Park. They were the most tender and vulnerable at bedtime. Sunkit, the bed-wetter, slowly drooped his eyes and then Zenky did as well and others asked for hugs, and all said "sweet dreams."

As I checked the girls, they were more settled but Rekhala needed a bandage due to the pencil sharpening project I had orchestrated to assuage the madness of the after-school study session. Then I spilled half a bottle of iodine all over her roommate Duma. They mothered themselves, but still wanted hugs and kisses and "sweet dreams." All around.

On my final round, I checked the café where I found the three bad girls, Murg, Panki, and Vindaloo, dancing and "helping Chef Chanda clean up," trying to cheat lights out. I shawled them, walked them back to bed and gave kisses and hugs. Panki, a twelve-year-old girl with a wandering eye, was a criminally insane kleptomaniac with a staph infection on her left heel, which she couldn't keep a bandage on through the day. Each night she would appear at the medical building with her tattered and dirty bandage barely clinging to her dust enshrouded foot, half wedged between ashy flesh and blackened "chapel" (the only shoe worn in India, the flip-flop).

They were all disillusioned and spoiled at the same time. They had taken trips to Australia, to Lassa to see the Dalai Lama, and also parts of Europe. They asked for things like they already had them. One girl, Jumla adopted me as her mother . She asked three times for my Pantene conditioner (a most prized possession as there was no conditioner in all of India that did not turn my hair to straw) and I gave it to her finally, painfully. The looks in their eyes said "You won't stay, why should I trust you?" as their mouths made the words, "I love you" and "Oh how beautiful you are" to get favors, gifts, reprieves from punishment, or special care.

But at the end of the day, they are good kids. Tricky, but good. Murg showed me by holding a long stick in her hand that was wedged into a pile of rubble, saying "Look, Ali, a pump!" as she cranked it up and down. She was showing me that she understood the machine lesson in the social studies class I had taught. My heart melted. They were both eager to please and be treasured yet naughty from the lack of strict and consistent parenting. I had to think, "Ah, a bit like myself!"

As I went to bed with dirty feet, hairy armpits, and most probably lice, listening to the mysterious, furious hiss at my window, searching for scorpions between the sheets, all I could think of was Zenky, a particularly wild, often in trouble showboat sort of a boy. When I had told the story of Jurassic Park I had named the boy Zenky and said he was greedy, unhappy with all his fancy pools, slides, and pets. He demanded only the extinct dinosaurs, causing his grandfather, Paolo (named for a long-term favorite volunteer/father figure here) to create Jurassic Park and for all the good dinosaurs as well as the bad. The good brontosaurus was Kuran named for a fourteen-year-old boy who sat at my feet studying English, a bit slow and demonstratively unloved. The bad velociraptor was Rabinder, named for the ten-year-old boy facing Zenky's feet that intently listened behind shy eyes (and would later be the donor of a "five-minute hug" on a particularly stressful day in the organic café). I concluded the story with Paolo swooping down from the sky in a helicopter to rescue our hero, Zenky from the ravenous, chomping teeth of Rabinder the velociraptor and the real boy Zenky added, as a moral to the story, "And Zenky was never greedy again."

Soon thereafter the mystery was solved. The hissing noise outside my window was a locust. I now understood why they are the purported harbingers of the Apocalypse. They are terrifying. The sound is something between a feral cat hiss and a parakeet gurgling. Mixed and alternating. It rattled like it had a wooden Times Square noisemaker lodged in its throat, and then it hissed like a cat when it's really mad. But actually I did become a bit worried about it, because after a while, its hiss had softened from ferocious to slightly desperate, like it had asthma and was gasping for air. I started to feel sorry for it, thinking maybe the cooler nights were starting to slowly kill it.

I almost quit over lice. I seriously thought about it. I mean who could fault me for saying, "I just don't want to have lice?" But I didn't and we established "delousing day" on Sundays. I bought combs in town and we took small groups to the guest houses where some of the volunteers stayed off-compound. I combed Jumke's hair a million times and couldn't rid her of the clinging white eggs until I scraped with my fingernails.

As I combed three more tiny, shiny black heads, the girls asked to have their hair cut and so I did. I did a very bad job and it came out very crooked, so I took them to the market to buy headbands and ear studs to disguise the chop job. We decided that after next week's delousing session, we would have ice cream. Lice and treats; the makings of an awesome tradition!

Then there were the giant black spiders. One right above my open suitcase. It was bigger than my hand, jet black and furry with an enormous body the size of a Kirby cucumber. It slinked silkily along the wall toward the door, maybe recognizing my discomfort. It crawled the length of my doorjamb, with me swishing a scarf at its behind, and tried to squeeze through the crack between the hinges, but it didn't fit. At that point I sympathized with it, because it seemed to be honestly trying to remove itself as the source of my terror and yet it thought it could squeeze into a spot it had, alas, outgrown. It then gracefully ducked out of its too-tight-squeeze, the doorjamb, and crawled down to the floor, then outside. I shrieked in spite of its clumsy grace.

Having heard my scream, Gopala laughed and said in his French accent, "Ah, big spider, big spider! Yeah yeah." I could tell he meant that it was harmless. Apparently they don't bite.

I met a woman in town named Mary who was all dressed in white and apparently awaiting a sadhu (perpetual spiritual student) friend of hers to come down from his mountain cave so she could ask him to marry her so she could obtain legal papers to stay in India. That was against his beliefs and he later left in a spiritual huff. But she told me something good, she said, "I came to India to lose my mind and what it has taught me is that I must beat down my spoiled inner brat."

I had first gotten a glimpse of this while still amongst the initial whirlwind: urged to use the bathroom without the use of toilet paper (Prabha would scoff and roll her eyes at Westerners and their toilet paper), unable to shower (cold water, teenage girls locking me out, dirty floors, mud and toothpaste all swishing underfoot in the wet-room style bathrooms), itching from bites, three days with no sleep, the hissing noise, chaos, uncertainty, non-acquaintance with the rules and routine yet still responsible for sixty kids.

I was uncomfortable, raw and shaky. I was walking to the Ganga in a gaggle of children, one girl holding my hand. She tugged and pulled and grabbed and I held on for dear life as my flip flops finagled the slippery slope. Her name was the river's name and she showed me how to run fast even as feet belied the safety there. Then, when at the water washing my clothes, Rekhala danced with me and allowed me to wash her mud-caked, favorite sweater; she attempted to teach me the classic Indian dance moves which she could expertly execute at age eight, her two-foot-high body writhing from the hips and twisting at the ankles and wrists. I couldn't keep up.

Then, poor Jumke climbed on my back to keep warm, her body drenched from dipping in the Ganga fully clothed.

Teeth chattering as I carried her up that treacherous hill, she said, "You are soooooo sweet!" And Sarita came to my room with red eyes, tilting her head back to allow me to apply my allergy eye drops. Monica came to the garden with me to "give love" to the plants I helped to plant. We said "give love" as we cupped our hands at our hearts in a scoop, then threw the love towards the many blooming plots in that garden, its soil fluffy from digging, tilling, then carefully, row by row, transplanting the delicate sprouts of lettuce from their birth bed to the garden, watering the buds in their new home.

It hit like a flash of lightning as my heart glowed orange, who's helping who here? It hit me that, from that first laughing Osho meditation where my tears flowed from images of pain, the five-year relationship and engagement lost, my restaurant mourned, my beloved New York City left, maybe even a lifetime of living for others from old scripts, living destructively from my script as a drunken brat. Here I was being healed. Simply put, their smiles, their hugs, their joy in song and dance along with India's purifying chaos was awakening something in me.

Every night at seven thirty we had satsung (Indian traditional prayer sitting); we sat in a the yoga hall all together in a huge, layered circle and chanted with our hands together, swaying back and forth, reciting the Hanuman Chalisa (the sacred song of Hanuman, the Monkey god) and other songs, like "You are my Sunshine."

The children taught me how to do laundry without heat and a machine, to not fear dirt, make due with what you have, value the smallest of things like a piece of string, a clip, or an old cloth that can be torn into rags to clean with. The children taught me true teamwork; each of us washed our own plates after meals, and all looked after each other. The children taught me freedom; no one needed ever to be too on time to anything, so you came willingly early most of the time. The children taught me simplicity and self-sufficiency, including self-soothing, like splurging on Skippy peanut butter, a chocolate bar, or mixed nuts. The children taught me how to live in the moment, hugging constantly and truly appreciating what you have right now.

My India looked like this:

Riding on the back of a scooter, looking out over a bridge onto a wide dried up riverbed, which gets flooded during the monsoons, but now is a desert of rubble and waste, trash, and shanties. There are fifty horses, running, eating, walking and lying down in a brown speckled pattern.

There are two wild boars grunting and running, their little, bloated, brownish-black bodies bouncing make me laugh and think of Pumba from The Lion King. Then there is a cow, not deigning to associate with the scruffy river rats below the bridge, just sitting casually in a heap against the bridge's cement rail, swatting irrelevantly at the hundreds of flies icing his white, regally humped back.

Three women sit against the railing farther down, like bums on the ground, but in richly colored saris, purple, silver, gold and fuchsia, feeding each other food from their hands.

I hear you God. I saw you in the bleeding sun trail across Mother Ganga, in the palm shrub on the hill, where one live tree thrusts tall and one dead creaks out like a crone's fingers. And in the small birds' shadows and sandy banks being lapped at by river ripples, the multiple smoke stacks from various rubbish-burning fires, the noisy rumbles and surpassing quiet, and a raft floating listlessly by.

The children's laughter echoing eternally in my heart. Thank you, Ramana's Garden; there I let go and allowed the reboot of my life to begin, to restart this viral hard drive of mine.

BAGGAGE AND GOD

December 2012

So, here's what happened yesterday. I'd taken an eight and a half hour overnight bus out of Rishikesh into Delhi, VIP seats and caretaking arranged by Nanda, then waited four hours in the airport to fly to Kathmandu, which was a brief and perfect jaunt of two hours on my new beloved Indigo airlines. I arrived around noon, my first time ever in Nepal. I was tired.

Off I went. I let this young Filipino man, my plane seat neighbor, talk me into sharing a taxi with him from the airport to find a guest house. When I arrived, I was doing really well, taking my time, exchanging money slowly and carefully, getting a quick photo for the Nepali visa, gliding through customs gracefully, as per usual. Then I went to collect my luggage.

Here's where, if it were a movie, the soundtrack would have jolted to a stop. We would have been watching perfectly softly scored Zen travel, a flute perhaps, or oboe--riding on the bus, noticing familiar Hindi words, names like the children had at Ramana's, which was now like family, sitting back on the luxury bus, in style, the driver having been tipped by my future, short-term husband to take care of me. Then flying cheaply and perfectly on that polished and coiffed Indigo airlines, arranged by Raj, Nanda's travel agent buddy. Then the Zen music would have crescendoed into orchestral reverie, full on cellos and violins, nay, fifty strings exploding like lotuses in ecstasy for the airport scene as I read Eat, Pray, Love and had divine realizations, profound moments of bliss, healing of my past. Then the music would have slightly rolled in denouement with my excellent meditation on the plane and calm arrival in a new and strange country, ready for the world. Then - BLGGGGRRRRRRRTTT (that sound when the record comes to a screeching, winding down halt).

Flow stopped. My baggage appears on the conveyor belt. I had started on this journey with a gigantic, red, rolling suitcase, half of CVS in its outer, bulging zipper pocket. It had popped a wheel in Delhi as I tried to race toward my ordinary bus, not having been able to muster the foresight that India did not value the elimination of bumps and damage in their roads and parking lots.

I'd bought this army backpack in Rishikesh for my trip to Nepal, thinking it ever-so-svelte an upgrade. Now it rolled forth, covered in laundry detergent (the kids call it washing powder), the small plastic Tide bag seeping out of my svelte army backpack's top compartment, which was supposed to be like some covert, secret pouch for grenades or hunting daggers.

But it was not staying latched, so it was now converted to an explosion of terrorist-looking powder and lame, limping trash. Then I tried to put it on and fell over backwards, to the ground. I leaned my foot on the conveyor rail and bent my torso parallel to the ground to get it on my back, got one arm in and it rolled off to the left with a resounding thud.

Finally, I wiggled my way into it laboriously somehow and put my small red Jansport backpack on my arms, facing front like a pregnant lady. I grabbed another brown bag I had, a Stella McCartney. Then I shouldered my purse and began to wobble to the exit where I was immediately confronted by yet another security check with a scanner belt. I unloaded, got scanned, reloaded, and continued clumsily to the airport's exit.

There my seatmate was waiting graciously with his tiny little, Everest-climber-looking turquoise, REI pack, asking if he could help me with my bags. He had already pre-paid a taxi to Thamel, the tourist part of Kathmandu where I was not going to stay because I had the inside scoop that Freak Street was the "real Kathmandu." But I abandoned my Freak Street plans and got a local, Nepali SIM card for my little Samsung cell. I ecstatically handed over my baggage to the strong hands of this trekker from the Philippines.

We went first to this horrible guest house, decorated with hundreds of empty beer bottles and assorted junk, looking like the trash yard from Sanford and Sons. We then went to a half-decent hotel that we agreed on and got two rooms side by side. I was scared. My fear painted pictures of roofies, stealthy organ stealing, and passport abstraction.

After settling into the room, he disappeared, so I went off to find the visa office, alone and wondering now if he hated me for my pathetic bag packing and didn't want to be associated with such un-travel-worthy company. I found the office and some sketchy-looking men. They took my passport, supposedly to go to the embassy, and disappeared for two hours. I was sure they were stealing my identity and I was planning how to get the police, cause a scene, get free, get myself back, get out – Get Out – GET OUT!!!!!

All of a sudden, the smarmy visa expediter guy came back with the threat that I would now have to wait two months to get back to India and could only get a three-month visa. But with his excellent services, smooth talk and finagling--phew – there was a chance I could maybe, just maybe, at the low low cost of two hundred and fifty dollars for him and his loyal tea-chugging, sleazy-looking, mean-laughing cohorts, I might have a chance. I grabbed my passport and, ever the Southern girl and hospitality-industry spell breaker, smiled and escaped their thievish plan.

Then my one India purchase, a gorgeous and heart-wrenchingly unique, one-of-a-kind necklace broke. And so did my laptop.

It was time for a reboot. Time for a restaurant.

I found a place called Black Olives in twenty steps and within a few moments was sitting in the sun reading my Kindle, sipping masala chai, awaiting Tibetan momos with chile sauce, on the side. Heaven, as always, was within reach.

Baggage and God

I slept like a baby from nine p.m. to nine a.m. and awoke with a new outlook on the Universe. I took a rickshaw to Freak Street, found a café that made New York-style cappuccinos, found a new guest house, and bought a sweater.

That's when it hit me: I hated my baggage because I hated the stuff in it. I'd held onto a lot of stuff because I had been in survival mode for most of my childhood; I acted like a five-year-old in part because that was the age at which I was molested by my best friend's father. I had not even absorbed the earth-shattering ramifications of that until, after having told my Aunt Betsy in my cousin's bar recently, she had, for the first time ever, the actual appropriate response of "Oh my God, Ali," bursting into tears and grabbing me tenaciously. But I don't need to carry that in my bags, or hold onto too old T-shirts, six or seven sleep shirts, or ugly clothes I hated in New York that I packed because they fulfilled Eastern standards of ankle and shoulder coverage.

I am me, exactly me, here and now, and I am being given a gift by Nepal to love myself exactly as I am. To throw away T-shirts, stained clothes, and realize that I do not need to keep anything I hate.

I made a plan immediately to donate clothes to the poor, mail ill-fitting cashmere sweaters, lotions, and valuables back to the orphanage, and discard trash.

I loved my squishy belly and my bravery at having eaten a hamburger the night before, quenching my protein-deprived body, soothing my cow-meat-loving soul. I loved that I was writing, everything that my mind and eyes touched wanted to be explored and caressed with words, like that is my secret prayer, divine communion with my world, the holy sanctifying act of gratitude that I had been denying myself for years. I cried and breathed and found God in the lightening of my baggage.

CHRISTMAS SAFARI

Chitwan, Nepal, December 2012

"In the jungles of India they call me Bagheera," began my favorite childhood story. I would listen to that scratchy Disney album over and over, in my Jungle Book trance, as if some part of my soul were traveling to a long ago but not forgotten home. In the jungles of Chitwan, in Sauraha, Nepal, I found that home.

It's Christmas Eve and by 6:00 a.m. we are on a canoe ride in a dugout tree heading down a water cabbage-covered river. Starlings sluice the cottony air as ruddy shelduck geese coo like nursing infants and the silky slide of the oar sings softly into the mist enfolding my meditation.

Later, we take a safari walk during which my small group is instructed to run to escape wild boar. We emerge into a broad field where hundreds of spotted deer nibble on dewy grass in the light-spackled clearing. Ground softly rumbles when they flee at our steps. At one point we encounter a rhinoceros that sees us. The guide instructs us into nearby bushes only later telling us we almost died and, "Sorry," because he is new and that should have never happened. "Beeeery Danger!!! Rhinoceros."

Finally, our walk empties into the elephant bathing site on the broadest point of the river. The guide tells us we can take an elephant shower now and it is perfectly safe. I heard one man died doing this last year. When inquire into this the elephant handler says not to worry, he was a mean and fat, Indian man from London, who kept clawing up the elephant's side repeatedly even when told to stop. He finally fell down and the elephant rolled over and sat right on top of him. "But don't worry, you nice lady!"

I delicately climb aboard, bare feet flat on strong curling trunk, hands holding his ears which have been proffered forward; we rise slowly like an escalator. I straddle this massive heap, these leathery tons. His name is Bambuchkali and he gently accords me his rough, rippling back; his coarse black hairs prickle my calves. I grab hold of his neck and as I do, I notice a neon green and black string laced through his right ear.

I wear the same exact necklace around my neck. This is a cheap, nylon bit of string only purchasable at temples and is worn as good luck by locals. I bought mine at Pashupatinath, a Hindu temple on the bank of the Bagmati river, where Nepalis burn their dead. This was one of many jarring cultural shocks, veering through bodies soaked in yak butter, ablaze on the sacred river bank and having wares and offers of service constantly pushed in my face.

The string connects us and eases my fear but I am not prepared for the shock that comes next as gallons of icy

Christmas Safari

cold water spray me. The winter here may not be as cold as perhaps I am used to. There is no snow or sleet or even gray sky, but it is crisp and windy and all of the other eleven tour group members have opted out of this part of the tour. But I was prepared. I had fled Kathmandu as my lungs began to get what tourists commonly refer to as "Kathmandu cough," diesel inspired and constant indoor smoking fired; my lungs had felt crowded. And so had my head. And it was Christmas so to escape my misery I took a guided tour, even though that was against my religion, and ventured here to Chitwan on "Safari."

From the moment the guide had given the introduction to our fun-filled weekend, he'd mentioned that there may be the possibility of an elephant shower on the last day. I had carefully queried how I might partake, what I should do and if anyone had died. I had prepared by wearing REI thermal, quick-dry leggings and easy to remove shoes. But when the brittle water pounds into my face, the wall of needles is proof that there are some things in life that no amount of preparation can amply ready you for. But as the shock subsides, I feel the magnificent clarity that comes from pure joy and newness. My skin is tingling as Bambuchkali jiggles a bit and reloads his trunk—another fire hose of chill! I squeal like a little girl and laugh myself alive.

After lunch we go for a long elephant ride called a "safari" (as we are looking for the ever illusive tiger I am fine to have never encountered). As I climb the rickety pine steps half tied with bamboo twine to a tree, supporting a wobbly platform jutting toward a saddled elephant, a flimsy box seat on its back, I notice the same necklace from my shower benefactor. Sure enough, it is the same elephant,

Bambuchkali! My friend is destined to be my Ganesha, my sacred remover of obstacles and a wind of much needed change in my life.

In the four hour jungle exploration we see five rhinos, which up close look like huge armadillos with goat hooves and a dinosaur-like horn. This time we are not in danger because of our dominant ride. They have the crinkliest butts you could ever imagine, their tails creased irretrievably between prehistoric, bumpy cheeks. We again encounter wild boar; this time a herd stops our tracks. "Shhhhhhhh! Be veeeeery quiet and DON'T MOVE," the guide says. He explains that they are the only animal in the jungle that can kill the tiger. "Beeeerrrry danger!" I don't quite believe him but remain silent nonetheless.

Riding on an elephant's back makes the world look smaller, more doable. In relation to the sheer sturdiness, the tons of languid anvils below my dangling form, all other matters seem minute. I am an Indian princess traversing her lands. I am Tarzan, swooping through the air with the drooping vines, the sun squinting through the dense, green, enshrouding foliage. I am Ernest Hemingway at the base of Kilimanjaro. I am at home in this jungle and in love with Bambuchkali.

It is such a solid and rolling ride; it goes a-thud-a-bump, ka-chunk-ka-chunk as his feet make dents in the ground beneath us and he unearths whole saplings with his writhing trunk for snacks. Insects hum like a heartbeat. Birds caw. I have found my home from my childhood story. It is like I have always known it. Something in my bones goes, "Aaaaaaaah." This is where I belong.

The world feels so alive. I take out the ring I bought in Kathmandu, Indian diamonds in two floral clusters of seven surrounding an Australian opal in a swirling Nepali gold setting. When I saw it I immediately knew it was the ring I had always so nebulously fantasized some soul-mate might proffer in his beginning efforts to swoop me away on his white horse. But now I place it on my own finger and I say, "With this ring I thee wed, to have and to hold, in sickness and in health, and death shall never do us part." For Christmas I declare loyalty to myself and with it a promise to always unite with the Divine that constantly surrounds us, especially in Chitwan.

DIFFERENCES

India, May 2013

Differences are more pronounced here. The caste system lies dormant under folds of wasted villages, ignored like babies on doorsteps, incubating in heat and ignorance. Even in the forward reaching cities like Mumbai and Delhi where old-school Hindus sport shorts and tanks like Westerners, the memory of that system, though faintly hidden (beneath veils of makeup, false smiles, diamond-dotted third eyes and gold jewelry), still sluices through the disguise with upturned noses at our wild Western ways, their searing eyes regarding our freedom disdainfully, our non-Hindu prancing.

Mom and I drive to a famous jungle spot for safaris and massages. She has come to join me for three weeks of my six month exploration, do the Taj, visit the Dalai Lama, Safari and raft down the Ganga. She practically had to drag me away from Ramana's Garden, where I had been living and working for four months when she arrived.

As we ride in our chauffeured Jeep, children run beside it as it plows carelessly past decrepit shanties. They trot by in once fancy dresses, blue chenille stained brown by dust, dotted with rhinestones and trimmed in dirty lace. Boys pull at a tree branch, desperately trying to dislodge its fruit, faces caked with dirt.

Water is scarce, and although the aqueduct we just traversed funnels flow off the Ganga, I am told that it is to provide electricity for the better off, to air condition high-rise luxury apartments. It is like men have channeled a leg off the Ganga in the same way the breast of Sati was cut away from her Shiva-grieved body, bits and pieces of her dispersed to the Earth.

Money divides us worldwide, separating our driver from us right now. This is the first time I have ever had a "driver," but I have to admit, after the bumpy, dusty Delhi ordinary bus, I am enjoying it. As much as we can be friendly, buy our driver, Rashid, lunch, eat together and try to bond, at the end of the day, Rashid is driving and we are paying. The staff at Hotel The Great Ganga, the beautiful hotel we stay in in Rishikesh, jump up when we cross any threshold to greet us. They never take a day off.

When I wonder what to do or say about this divide in culture, in socio-economic gaps, ensuant judgment or fear, the Universe sends me a message. As we approach the Taj Mahal, there are many Muslim structures in the surrounding area. My instinct says "No, I want nothing to do with anything Muslim right now." But the Universe says, "Go."

So I do. I tour the tomb of Akbar; my heart opens to its beauty. I see clearly how it is not a love tribute, but

Differences

a contrition monument. I fall in love with the ornate gilding in stones and the craftsmanship which overlays the arc entrance, carnelian, malachite and onyx. That is the answer to any divide in our All Oneness. And it is all I can do; embrace the Divine as it embraces me, without prejudice and colored foresight, remain open and inquisitive to the best of my ability, and relate equitably to all of life as it presents itself. Bridge the differences in my own heart whenever I can.

Shiva Temple

Odanaku, Nepal, Nanda's village, July 2013

At Ramana's Garden, I had hoped to become the next Mother Teresa or some such ego-fulfilling madness where I could pinpoint what I was rebooting my life for, what I was destined to become.

Instead I fell in love with the brother of the mother of Monica, the little girl whom I had taught to "give love" in the garden and to whom I had bequeathed my favorite earring. I was looking for recovery from my five-year, verbally abusive relationship. I began to feel my withered roots grow buds, then, in typical alcoholic fashion; I jumped into engagement with him, with Nanda. But first, on the back of his motorcycle while courting clandestinely in Rishikesh, so his Hindu boss didn't see him (because he would be disappointed that I was not a Hindu girl and fire him, supposedly), I promised Nanda that I would return to visit his village in western Nepal, in the Kalikot District. If I had known what I was getting into, I would have never done it.

The village, Odanaku, was a two-day hike from where the bus was supposed to drop you off, however; in my case, the bus stopped short due to landslides and muddy roads (which was a welcomed relief after ten hours traveling precariously on what National Geographic dubs "the world's most dangerous road," with long drops straight down, narrow curves, and sometimes even roaring rivers).

We did not make it to the Kalikot District that night because my legs turned to butter about halfway up what I felt to be the side of a mountain, stepping up boulders two and three feet high. After three and a half hours of that, my knees crumbled beneath me and the tears began to flow even though I had promised Nanda I would never cry or scream on the mountain. He begged a lower caste family to put us up, which was apparently difficult to do as they were afraid of their involvement in bringing shame upon him, a higher-caste man. As I watched the debate, I sat leaned against a mud house, too tired to eat, freezing, and drenched with sweat, wondering why I had come.

They fed us and put us up on two tiny wooden platforms covered by bedbug infested blankets. The next day we walked all day, and then slept again in muddy, itchy quarters. I got blisters from my new hiking boots and popped them, thinking it would help with the excruciating pain (I had iodine and Neosporin and Band-Aids on them). But they, instead of healing, due to lack of water and constant walking in feces-filled dirty paths wearing only sandals in the village, turned gangrenous, two black silver-dollar-sized welts stolidly implanted in the arches of my feet so that I was sure I would lose them.

The last leg of the journey was straight up. By the time I arrived, I felt like I had done some kind of interplanetary travel and entered an inner fold, removed from the realm of regular existence. But I was too numb, confused, and tired to notice its magnificence. The glowing emerald shelves of rice paddy fields, nestled in the nooks of Himalayan heaven, wet, misty and crystal-air coated, floating amongst the clouds. But I never was able to breathe it in, not until I was leaving, after five long weeks of staying with his family and often being alone with people who couldn't speak a word of English, trying desperately to connect.

A few days in, Nanda warned me that the biggest festival of the year was coming and that he may have to leave me for some time. I asked my tricky Nepali what this meant because I had come to learn that the truth was a slippery slope, that reality seemed to morph according to the moment, and that perceptions change things. He said, "Oh maybe, like, eight days." I know now that he was preparing me for the worst so he had some wiggle room for a few other options.

I tremored at the thought of being left without my friend and soon-to-be husband in this strange land where the culture was already terrifying and overwhelming me. When I had tried to be a part of a party for a new baby I had felt compelled to help, wanting to accompany my fiancé to get the wood to build the stupa-like structure that guests would pass through, he scoffed that women could not do this and he would be laughed at if I tried. I should stay and help with chapatti (a hand patted bread of simple brown flour and water, cooked over an open fire) with all the other squatting women. We fought and he asked if he should take me down the mountain immediately. Not wanting to be ejected, I made a concerted effort to fit in.

When my time of the month came, it happened to be my birthday and I had to abide by some of the "small house" rules that the thwarted, ancient village Hindus still cling to. What this means is a woman is supposed to be kept in the barn during her period, with the goats, chickens, and cow shit. She is not to touch anything that could touch anyone else, like plates, spoons, or pots. She must separate in all ways. For meals, she is served by a ladle that is conspicuously held a certain amount of uncontaminating inches above her plate. She is given her own pitcher with which to wash her plate and keeps all eating tools separate from her family's, or host's, in her room.

I was to keep all my things separately in my room. I was allowed to stay in the room and not sleep in the dung and hay but we had to have a priest come after seven days and do a puja (a spiritual cleansing ritual) to purify the space. I had to pay him forty dollars and empty out the contents of the room. He then built a fire on the dirt floor and performed the cleansing ceremony with an elaborate sand, stone and marigold mandala. Then we washed all the material from the emptied belongings, all clothing, blankets, even thick rugs. It was awful enough in theory, but in practice it was like having my humanity taken from me, as if I were sludge at the bottom of the barrel. To be untouchable, to be paraded through the village to wash every other day publicly so they knew; to wash all the clothes I had in the tiny little trickle that was the tap for the entire village was like wearing the scarlet letter.

When Nanda tried to explain why I would never make it to the Shiva Temple, I was in no mood to buy his tricks or to be left behind. I insisted on going. I trained for eight days, walking three to six hours every day up those steep, craggy cliffs, in crevices that could never be deemed trails, over slippery rocks still wet with water's kiss and up over stones requiring again, two to three foot high steps.

Drenched in sweat every day, my spirit was caught somewhere between demolition and determination and I resorted, as I do, to constant private prayer. Shiva told me he wanted me to come and that he would help me up if I just kept going as I had been, not to worry, his hands would be under me if I only but tried.

The day finally came and we walked only a few hours the first day. Another fact my future bigamist had neglected to tell me was that we were to fast the day before and the day of the trek for Shiva. Thank God their version of fasting included eating shiau and kakro (apples and cucumbers).

On the day before I impressed his entire family by helping to paint the whole house green with Nanda and Uncle Dam. Bajai (grandmother) was particularly inspired by my fortitude which helped counterbalance the awful impression I had created from my bad "small house attitude." When I was being treated like a leper I had pounded my dishes (which I had to keep separate from theirs) against the wood railing over which I washed them out, clanging my distaste upon her watchful, reproachful eyes, as she squatted, always squatted and smoked hashish.

We arrived the first night of the trek to a tiny dirt house in the middle of a field. It was cold and drizzly and my legs were once again butter, my insides quaking. I was dizzy with exertion and in a dreamlike state of non-attachment to physicality.

A young woman served us the best chai I have ever tasted. It seemed the epitome of Ayurvedic medicine as my husband-to-be told me the herbs in it were ancient Himalayan healing cures from nearby in these hills. It tasted like fairytale, like incense inspired to holy.

Like stars thrown down by Vishnu into the bottom of a clear creek that had been eaten by some magical newt, then spewed out over hundreds of centuries into the snows of these mountains until some fair maiden with a pure heart called their twinkle to the surface. It made my insides tingle and spin with a deep down stirring as if these herbs were the only things ever to know exactly where into exactly you to reach.

Mami (Nanda's mother) had paid the girl three hundred rupees for me to sleep in her bed, the only bed, alone. The rest of our traveling band bunked upstairs in the attic lying on scarves and each other's stomachs. They danced and sang all the hours we attempted rest, so no one slept. The rain had caked the bed with mud from feet. There were fleas and eventually two other girls crawled into the tiny wooden bed and rolled me against the wall so tightly my chest compressed to breathlessness. At 2:15 a.m. Nanda told me to get up, and have chai. It was a dream as I struggled to find clothes that were dry, pee in the dark, and get back

Shiva Temple

on the trail by 2:45, armed with my headlamp against a wall of blackness.

We walked three hours in the pitch-dark and six more in the light. As the elevation increased to about 9,000 feet, so did the streams and the slopes. I had only the hands, Prakash's, Nanda's, Uncle Bir's (my favorite set of hands, steady, gentle) and Gagan's (my least favorite--I dubbed him "dead fish" because as I reached for his support, his hands would sink down in limp surrender). But with those hands I made it to the bottom of the final hill, "Maha Bouy," or "Mother Mountain."

It was on this mountain that a legendary Shiva lingam had supposedly thrust itself up out of the ground next to a sleeping hobo, who, hitherto deaf and dumb, became immediately healed and prolific in the ancient Vedic texts and all Brahmin knowledge. Here people had traveled from all over to ask Shiva for boons for their families. Nanda said everything he'd ever asked for had been granted. We bathed in the stream to purify for Shiva, splashing freezing cold water anywhere we could reach without revealing too much flesh, having peeled off treasured layers of clothing, then re-donning them for the forty-degree air, picking up all the offerings for Shiva, including prayer flags, bags of rice, reeds of grass, and goats (I bought one for sixty dollars and named her Sati, after Shiva's consort who had thrown herself on her father's fire, then been carried around the world until the other gods got impatient with him and Vishnu threw his wheel of creation to cut off her body parts, which scattered ceremoniously all over the world. They didn't seem to like that name).

Most of the women did not go any farther. They stayed at the base of this final peak to offer Prasad (used in both India and Nepal, a Hindu blessed candy or rice to put in your mouth as a blessing from the gods) to the pilgrims after they descended from the temple. The last climb was straight up a grassy hill at a seemingly seventy-degree angle. I had nothing left. Nanda's friend Depu had turned around and gone back down last year at this very point and he was a robust twenty-seven-year-old man. Shiva kept his promise to me though. It was as if I were held in a bubble in his hands. I felt mysteriously buoyed to the top, uplifted and carried on a cloud, lifted to a higher plain, literally.

No one could actually believe I made it, including myself.

So imagine my disappointment when my tricky Nepali said to me, "So, remember that part where I told you there was a ceremony where only I could go and you would have to stand back a little ways and just watch?" He had explained that as the male representative of the family, he went in and participated in a ritual where they all encircled the lingam, made their offerings and asked for their boons for the year. While we were walking up and I was panting and disoriented, he told me that he would walk in and I would stand just a little bit back, but could still see all that was going on.

"Yeah," I replied with trepidation.

"Well, there is the spot for you to stand," and he pointed his stubby, stupid ashen brown hand to the area where everyone removed and left behind their shoes before entering the sacred temple.

I crack and tears leak out. I felt such a heaviness for a country full of women denied entrance to the sacred by its scared and shivering, cowardly men, men who could make promises and then marry other women, men who could banish women to a "small house" during menstruation (probably just because they were frightened), men who could drink all day and night while their sari-covered wives could battle the fields and sun, or set themselves on fire as their only means of freedom.

When I had first arrived, the family had sacrificed a sheep in my honor, smearing its blood over the arched kitchen door to regale the community with their good fortune. I noticed this as I looked across the clay porch to see Auntie sitting in the rain with bits of hay in her hair. She was in her "small house" time, keeping her untouchable distance due to her life-giving blood, while the blood of slaughter arched violently above her own, off-limits kitchen door. Her two sons ran and played freely and cooked dinner, while she shivered in the wet and cold, dirty from sleeping in the barn.

And now here, at the top of a mountain, which it had taken a village and a blue god with cobras and a trident (Shiva) to lift me up onto, I stood alone and felt crushed. Little did I know that I was to become even more crushed as I was discarded a year later in Nanda's marriage to Sarita, supposedly by the insistence of his three-day wailing mother, who had called me daughter during my stay.

Later, on the way down, Nanda told me I had ruined this sacred day for him, one which had always brought him so much joy. He had begrudgingly offered to take me into the temple, if that was what I really wanted. I looked at the concerned faces of my new family who had helped me up that mountain and I could not go into the temple. They believed that to do so would bring a curse on the family of the woman who would dare be so brazen. The story went that a woman had stood up to Shiva asking, "Which is longer, your lingam or my hair?" and that Shiva had struck her dead on the spot and all women who entered would therefore suffer a similar consequence.

In return for my semi-graceful acquiescence, I asked him one small favor. I asked him to just to consider what I felt, that women were being put down by his culture, by this particular restriction especially, by being kept out of the temple.

"What does that mean, 'put down?'" he asked.

"Made to be less than," I replied. "The story you tell, of why women aren't allowed in the temple. About the woman challenging Shiva, don't you see that it paints women badly? You are supposed to be humble in front of God and what she has done is exactly the opposite?!"

He looked at me with bewildered eyes and promised to consider these things so he could get on with his ritual.

While he had entered the temple I had walked down to the base of the temple and sat in meditation on the grass with my own prayer. To God, to Goddess, Shakti, in all her forms, brutal Kali, masterful Durga, gentle Lakshmi, Compassionate Quan Yin, all aspects of the Divine in its many forms, even Shiva, the destroyer.

Shiva Temple

I asked that Nanda receive whatever it was he came here to request, which he told me was the success of our marriage plans, travel to America, and the start of our own tour business. In retrospect, I have no idea what it was he requested at that holy temple. It could have been for the family he has now with Sarita and his baby boy, David. Who knows? It could have been for the Oda Foundation, which an American brought to his village, which helps by building a medical compound for which Nanda is now accredited as basically a king. I asked that day for the healing of all women who are put down and sit outside the temple of the Divine.

Whatever I prayed for, and even though I only sat on the ground at the temple's base, something must have happened between me and Shiva, because nowadays I am able to pray for Nanda, wishing him, as we are taught in recovery, everything I would ever have wished for myself.

Steam Room

Back in the USA I still didn't know what to do with my life. Plus, everything was on hold while I waited for Nanda's fiancé Visa to be approved, which took five months and my mother's loving support and help from an immigration lawyer. I enjoyed the liminal state, sometimes feeling lost and loserly, sometimes profoundly inspired by future prospects.

Once I had an epiphany in the steam of the Cedar's, my stepfather's retirement community where I was living (against the rules) and loving it. God/the Universe and Everything could not have provided a better place to reenter from shanty yet chaotic India with jet lag and a lack of a life. I had water aerobics on Monday, Wednesday and Friday, lectures in the afternoons, including one by a nationally accomplished Audubon founder and Conservationist (he planted trees with two presidents and is going to save the world by encouraging us to buy shade-grown coffee, grown without decimating rain forests), went to the theater and had many meals in the elegant and excellently staffed restaurant (including a brunch buffet with waffles, carving stations, and multiple desserts), oh and I played a rockin' bocce ball! Picture if you will—I am in the pool with ten, seventy to eighty-year-old women and we are circling our arms underwater while holding these barbell-looking floaty things in simulation of a paddle motion, one over the other, and the instructor inspiringly yells out, "Okay guys, bring it home, last one!" and I love it. Finally, exercise I can handle!

The epiphany was that we simply travel in a bubble of energy and it is constantly in flux and morphing, like those huge bubbles created from soap, with swirling rainbows and clear walls, a huge transmogrifying landscape of the soul. We are constantly being inundated with these old swirls, the habits, the patterns that emerged in childhood as mechanisms to deal with the pain, survive hardships, or simply exist. They come into play like a constantly re-emerging broken record groove.

There is a green swirl of being overwhelmed as a girl who helped raise her mother, thinking I am not good enough to function in this world, to be paid, to be accomplished, to be good. For J, a red and black swirl of depression, a young boy who learned that life is hard by working on his farm and watching death and decay obliterate sustenance, who learned to crawl into a cave of inactivity or doom and gloom thinking.

A blue swirl of not enough-ness, a mother who never had time for her child and is constantly reverting to a possibility that there is something more to do. And just as there are backwards grooves, or ripples like that, there are also forward circles—ways of inhabiting our space in a fruitful, connected, positive-moving, interactive vein that furthers our passion and divine purpose. It all seems to be triggered by our actions and thoughts, how we feed our bubble with our daily activities, our patterns, the way we nurture ourselves, spend our time, show the Universe how our energy is meant to flow. And doing water aerobics is definitely adding positive streaks for me.

On the other end of the spectrum, I had lain on the couch only days before reading Elizabeth Gilbert, thinking I could never write and publish my book because what does the world want with Eat Pray Love 2? And how was I supposed to do my taxes? Where was my W-2 anyway? And where was my life? Was I an expat? Could I stand to relocate? Am I a bum? Do I only have monetary value in the world as the slave to others/restaurant grinder that does work that gradually peels her soul off layer by layer?

As I walked past the daffodils that lined the trim, retirement home sidewalk, I noticed that the first one I came across was the most perfect specimen of yellow and pale flower I had ever seen, like a cloud or an angel; the next however, and the five that followed it, were a disgrace to their kind. They were withered unrecognizable and crying to have their sad crusty heads chopped off in order to put them and their viewers out of misery.

But they were all part of the greater story, and could even exist in my newfound Utopia. Alas, it takes it all kinds and we all find our niche under different circumstances and beds of soil that we make and lie in, and cultivate.

In the steam, I had turned it to "High" so it scalded my shin skin. In a sweat lodge-type prayer, I emitted my perpetual call to the great spirit, "How may I be of service...Thy will, not mine, be done."

I heard the faint reply of, "It is easier than you believe. You are stronger than you think. God is here more than you realize."

And then I gradually translated that to, "It is easier than I believe. I am stronger than I think. God is here more than I realize."

And then simply to, "It is easy. I am strong. God is here."

And with that, I received an enthused (which from the Greek literally translates to "to be inspired by a God") reinvigoration to write. And to just be me, in my beautiful, constantly re-perpetuating bubble of beauty; to look out at the world from that as much as possible, and see what I see.

Recovery Table

For a while, it was good, bringing my Nepali to America, tricky liar that he was and all. We first lived in a tiny one-bedroom apartment with my mom and stepfather (a transitional apartment on their way to their own condo as the assisted living one had been more for his wife who had died of Parkinson's). He worked construction and I cooked all day, fresh food, homemade Nepali bread. Then we had the best wedding ever. We kayaked in on a lake behind my mother's Oriental home.

My best friend wrapped me artfully in a sari Nanda had sent me from Rishikesh, on top of the Japanese, red-painted bridge, with all eyes watching, to a sitar Pachelbel Canon. We married in a Quaker circle with an Episcopalian priest blessing us to high heaven and my brother friend's mother officiating in all her India-loving glory. Another best sister-friend made a cake with calla lilies and the Sanskrit symbol for the highest form of love. The cake was purple and four-tiered, lovely orange and chocolate inside.

But eventually it all came crashing down after he returned to his village, Odanaku for a two-month visit and ended up marrying a Nepali woman, the nurse with the Oda Foundation. But he had dragged me to a new place in North Carolina that I never knew, Saluda, where I'd helped get him a job as a kayak guide on the Green River. We lived in a cabin above a wild mountain woman who we adopted as Auntie. And I joined a fine recovery circle in Hendersonville, where I belong to this day. Being a part of it brought me back to a memory from New York, with a gentle reminder of how far I've come, the gratitude I have, and how far I've yet to go….

New York City, September 2009

There's an unmistakable charge of energy in a busy restaurant, the clang of plates being thrown into a bus-bin, the jangle of glasses fresh from the dishwasher, safe in their compartmented rack, shimmering with sanitizer. There's a buzz-hum of mixed voices, satisfied and conversing, also hungry and babbling, the swish of the staff's legs as they fly from here to there in multitask frenzy. I gloried in it.

One Thursday in particular I remember that feeling flowing so fully, I made myself stop hustling for a minute and stand still in my tracks, the fanned out cuffs of my brown polyester suit still swaying, my arms crossed. I took a breath and drank in the energy of a successful, churning restaurant. Everything flowed with purpose, burbled with its ability to create perfect hospitality.

Johann, my assistant manager/sometime server was the only fixed point, his hands resting on his brown-apron-clad waist amidst the whirlwind, wiping beads of sweat from his fuzzy, balding head. I wondered what pills he was on tonight. Zuri sped past, a party of five in tow. She fastidiously rigged two four-tops together to accommodate them and I flew in to help so that she didn't scrape the floor or, as often occurs, let the guests assist.

"Ah ah ah! You're not allowed!" I twittered, as a husband arched over and extended his arms, about to lift with his back and not his legs!

From the corner of my eye, I felt a swarm of bees encroach like a giant inky blob seeping in. I looked over to see Earl, Mary, Sophie, John, Henry, and five others approaching.

"Is it Thursday already?" I shouted with my "Good grief, Charlie Brown" hands in the air. A joke I loved, but wasn't sure anyone else found amusing.

"So, it's ten tonight, huh?" I queried, neatly nodding to my chef and right-hand-man, Guillermo, who'd bet eight, while Zuri had bet six. I'd won again. It was a game we played to keep spirits up before the rush came, when we doubted it ever would–betting on the numbers of the two regular large groups we had: Tuesdays the bell ringers from Trinity Church and Thursdays, the drunks, fresh from a meeting.

Zuleikha was new so I had to explain, "Okay now, when you serve this group, you have to get bread on the table ASAP because they're all alcoholics and they're pissed off that they can't drink so they feel really hungry and we have to head 'em off at the pass. Oh, and go ahead and bring everyone water–with lemon! They have to have something to drink!"

Krishna, the busser, already had the rolls in the pizza oven warming and four silver wire baskets ready to put on the tables, but I could see Zuleikha thinking that was enough, so I shouted over the bar, where I was running to make a specialty cocktail, "Olive oil and butter!" She nodded comprehension and, satisfied, I set to my task of muddling oranges and fresh mint with Cointreau, smelling their flavor magically open up and meld to create my own concoction called the Mojo-jito, a gourmet orange mojito.

I'll never forget how angry I got when Mary, a pretty brunette at the recovery table, petite and birdlike in appearance, turned into a complete monster toward my oldest serve, Monique. She was shouting at her, standing up in her face and pointing wildly to the line. I intervened and asked her to please not talk to my staff like that, to calmly tell me what was wrong so I could fix it.

"That burger has been sitting there on that metal shelf for fifteen minutes and your server refuses to bring it to me. I even saw her glance at it and walk right past it like she didn't even care! I'm starving, but I'm sure it's well done now and I'm so fucking pissed off, I don't even want it!" She'd done a really good job with the calming down part.

I assured her I wanted nothing but her happiness and would cook her a burger to perfection myself (which meant Guillermo would and I would say I did to show her how selfless and sacrificing her dire need made me be). As soon as we put it on the grill, I buttered her up while she waited, as we had Super-Vulcan, the double broiler doing the dirty, heroic deed (an extremely high temperature grill which heated from above and below). I brought her more water and put a hand lightly on her shoulder. "Look, I promise you it will be ready shortly; our grill is running at about eight hundred degrees right now and your medium rare will only take three and a half more minutes. And it is so delicious and juicy; it will be well worth the wait!"

Inside my head I'm thinking, "Fucking miserable drunk. Just have a shot of vodka–you'll feel better." I see Monique muttering under her breath as her eyes veer in our direction, so I swoop over and remind her, "Hey, we don't ever disparage our guests (while we are here) no matter what! Okay?" I wait for her disgruntled nod and faint hint of a forced smile as I beeline to the line to pick up my rush burger refire and then it hits me; somewhere deep inside I'm secretly rooting for Mary, perhaps even jealous.

Two years later when we are still serving them their immediately warmed dill rolls and expedient waters with lemon, I notice that Mary doesn't have quite such an edge. She is serene, nay, even kind.

Saluda, August 2014

When I was twelve, I wanted to be the youngest published author. I went to Duke Young Writers' camp five summers standing and was enamored of every aspect of being a writer, the smell of the paper, fresh and waiting for words, the click of a pen, poised and prepared to make them. I loved making sentences sing and painting pictures of the world that could maybe, just maybe, capture the beauty I saw in it. It was my biggest dream. I filled sixty-five journals. At age seventeen, my boyfriend Scott often remarked, "You know, Ali, you're gonna have to spend the last half of your life just reading about the first half."

Worried that might be true, I read them all when I first moved to New York. It took six months. I highlighted parts that I thought might have promise. Unfortunately, only one-one hundredth of the ravenous devourer of my time was left twinkling in yellow and pink. Perhaps A Farewell to Arms was not in store, but maybe a small collection of chances.

Many dreams I've had have fallen to the wayside—movie star; hot, smarty pants lawyer; Amelia Earhart. I'd made it to New York City at least and that was always a big one. I'd made it there. Just surviving had been my goal. No more writer, no more actress, the title of New Yorker would suffice. Being the GM of my own New York City restaurant had filled me with pride. It was too bad that it led to burnout and a downward drinking spiral that almost killed me. But it was good while it lasted, while it worked, wearing my Brooks Brothers suit, eating oysters at Blue Fin, drinking champagne at the W, meeting colleagues at the Waldorf. All so amazing. Until it wasn't.

Maybe I was in love with New York because I knew it was gonna bring me to my knees, bring me tumbling down, all the way down the ladder my ego had crawled up, to realize one simple thing. I am an alcoholic. Now my biggest dream is being able to keep my side of the street clean, which for me involves doing the steps. In sobriety I get to feel things I never wanted to. And guess where I end up some Sunday nights? I meet up with a group of people who, like me, cracked their souls on the bottom of the bottle. We have a little meeting wherein every month that has five Sundays, we assemble a panel of old-timers (those with twenty years or more of sobriety) and they answer questions. After the meeting, we eat at O'Charley's down the street. We're a party of anywhere from six to twenty. We quibble over how many free apps we are entitled to get from our guest survey coupons, send our overcooked burgers back at a whim and, of course, enjoy the fresh rolls, still hot from the oven, with their accompanying butter and smiles from the reluctant server.

Blackbird

Saluda, January 2016:

"Life on life's terms" is what we call it.

What we mean is, just because we get sober doesn't mean we live on our newly discovered pink cloud on the heaven float of peachy forever and ever. Life will still be life, my sobriety endured in the face of hardship, discovering Nanda's bigamy on the internet. He had given me all his passwords to help him write responses both on Facebook and Google to prospective Doctors, Volunteers and Investors in Oda Foundation.

One lonely night working third shift at The Pavillion I had looked at his private Google photo uploads to discover him with this beautiful, yellow clad, square jawed Nepali woman pressed to his cheek. Then I searched his Facebook messages to discover one from his business partner inquiring when the wedding day was to be.

Right after that a doctor discovered a tumor in my intestine he said was cancer and I had to have a colectomy and resection to remove six inches of colon and put it back together. I survived and came out stronger than ever, but there were moments. Like the night I couldn't sleep, alone in Saluda, waiting out the year until I could file for divorce in the Polk County court.

"Blackbird singing in the dead of night…" The Beatles' song that I sang to him at our wedding shaking my core; I'd changed the words to "I was always waiting for this moment to arrive."

What are you doing, little girl? Up and singing into your phone when you should be sleeping? What are you doing sending a voice note to your husband's business partner on Facebook Messenger by accident? You sang to him on your wedding day, your heart spilling over, and tears in your eyes, that you were always waiting for this moment to arrive. And that he had waited for this moment to be free. His eyes had pooled with tears in response.

What are you doing, little girl? Up by candlelight trying to sing yourself to sleep with that song?

"You were only waiting for this moment to be free."

Thinking you could sing yourself to sleep? Thinking when you shouldn't be. Thinking when you know it only sets your head on fire when you know you should be instead soaking your heart in the cool wash of restorative sleep. Where will this thinking get you? Sending out into the world the most vulnerable siren a girl could emit, sending out a call to the lonely, the yearning, the hurt, the preyed upon, sending out your song of release and of peace–but to the wrong person! Oh no, what have you done?! You are a wreck, a mess, a disheveled jumble of netted wires, a cross-firing distinction of woundedness, a disturbing interconnection of loss, weird, loony, unhinged, or is it just unbridled?

"You were only waiting for this moment to be free."

Hey, little girl, what are you doing? Creating some stain? Unleashing some beast? Unfurling upon the world the scraggly-haired, unkempt, pent-up little ruffian you have behind bars inside you? Is it forever? Did we break? Is all undone?

Wait. Shhhhh. No. I hear no cracking. No frozen ice sculpture splashing or crashing millions of trickles on the ballroom floor. I hear only night and the purr of the insects where they strum the darkness, a careful whir, streamlined clicking ricochets, gentle nudges, and high-pitched whistles like air through goddesses' harps to soothe her babies' broken hearts.

Nothing to do but let go. Nothing to do but wait. Remember that life, in part, is mess, chance, jump and mistakes. Not an easy slide. You always used to say to yourself if life were easy, it would be droll, because there would be nothing to compare joy to. Without heart-pounding, fingers-sweating trial, there would be no life, only play-acting empty sleeping charades. Be alive, be awake, be foolish. Be yourself–and scare yourself into the place where you need those harps. You know from the program that the only thing to do with pain and chaos and revolutionary disturbances is face them and turn them into peace. Serenity from calamity.

You were only waiting for this moment–to be free.

BATH

But there is hope; I learned that in the tub.

Saluda, January 2015

I have told myself so many bad stories. And continue to do so on a daily basis. At the age of five, my father read to me from The Hobbit as my bedtime story. One time, as he did so, he tweezed a tick from my back while holding a lit match to it. That, and only that, was love. I feasted hungrily on his words as he read about Bilbo and impersonated Gollum saying, "My precious."

This happened occasionally, during a once-every-three-months visit and I clung to that feast, an indulgence, as if I were starved. It became a thread in my tapestry. This glorious weaving of my life's story had within it, this central and controlling theme of love-hunger as its baseline, like a red color theme, the foundation for other tales to weave amongst.

Then there's the matching pink blush of unrequited love stories folded in like egg whites. A crimson shock of two date rapes at UNC and, oh yeah, one at work, on Christmas Eve at a seafood restaurant in Pasadena, CA by a Mexican prep cook named Jesus. Heartbreak and betrayal a repeating outline of black bordering many patches. And because this orchestration of color and texture wove a tale so beautiful and adorning, I kept them and added on to my gallery-worthy tapestry. We all develop a taste for a certain design or style that matches our experiences and the stories we create. We remain defined by the story and its baselines, all the same. In other words, these false ideas of our defining pains, what they say about the inadequacy of us become an easy go-to place for our future decisions, paths.

God says to release. Unravel story…Let it go.

Often in the bath, I unravel and release. Here is how one bath came to pass:

It is hot, almost too hot to touch; I boiled three huge pots of water to make it so and eased my body in slowly, feeling as if welts might arise in response to the hot sting of the water. I am steeping something out, sizzling away some pain. At first this was my ritual to try to get my husband out of my pores, my cells, my bones. I read about it in a spiritual book. It was a ritual one woman used to get over her ex. She wrote a thirty-page letter to him, saying anything and everything she ever possibly wanted to express to him, pouring out freely, dumping resentments, leaving pains unedited. Then she burned the letter and took a salt bath to imagine it all being sucked out of her, allowing herself to imagine him slithering down the drain with the water and away from her body, mind, and soul. She did this three times in a two-week period and felt relief; genuinely lightened and free. I wanted to feel that. So I did it three times too. Today was the fourth, only this time, there was no letter. I had said all I could, ridding myself of the words, the nasty spouts, rants, and rage; now there was only sadness.

I ease into the scalding water, seeking to tap into residual hurt from this man who left me to marry another woman, who seemed to have easily forgotten all about me. After a month with no contact from him, I felt like an insignificant feather on the wind, no more a part of his life than some fleeting thought or whim, not the major life choice and commitment he had been for me. But he is not there, inside me, in my bones and cells. He is gone. I have already washed him away and I feel the absence of him, a spacious freedom from his possession of me. It is amazing, but then I go deeper.

It is an epiphany, a flash of almost unavoidable awareness–that although he is not there, there are old scars, memories in my cells that have a tendency to grab onto new experiences and classify them as affirmation of the old ugliness. I can see them, these old memories or ideas. They have formed an actual force field in my physical being (in my legs and in my belly) which is waiting for new things in life to happen to mirror those old stories to prove an old pain anew. It is earth-shatteringly enlightening because suddenly I know that I don't have to do this. Simply noticing my tendency to do this creates power.

I remember when Jeffre, my chiropractor and a spiritual healer in Los Angeles, worked on me and I had a similar experience. As he worked on me, I saw these old traumas actually located in specific spots in my body as they were lifted up and released. For example, the trauma of Mom driving me to school and crying her guts out while screaming "life is so hard," lived in my thighs, these massive lumps of stone looming like a legacy of modern dance, biking, karate and fencing, but really being where I had to support myself and even her—too young. Jeffre was able to lift the story out, expose it for the illusion it was, the lingering idea of it, and therefore unravel and release its presence in my tapestry.

That was what this bath was for me. I knew that any new pain from Nanda having betrayed me had been relieved, but there were old stories in my skin, actual DNA remembering that Dad had abandoned us, that my first love had broken my heart and my second love too. And these woven-in reiterations of that baseline wanted to reassert the story of that wounding. But I didn't have to let them grab onto new experiences and make that proof that I could not change! It was my choice. I decided what things meant. I could see so clearly that peace is a choice, a moment-to-moment assertion I can make or avoid.

It is incredible how simple this seems in one nanosecond of ultimate clarity, but yet how elusive it can be to grasp living day to day. At the rehab center where I worked at the time of that bath, I developed a notion that I was nothing, a lowly chemical dependency technician on third shift who couldn't even get that job right. But if this lesson is true, then it doesn't really matter what I do, because all is perfect exactly as it is, it is only the story that I tell myself that matters, what threads I decide to weave into my new tapestry. Life is perfect. All that is left is to see it as such.

David

The funniest thing just happened. I just heard a new friend in recovery speak about the steps in a refreshing way, how they reminded her of that Michelangelo quote about David; he said, "I just chipped away all the rock that was not David." She said that we were doing that; in working the steps, we reveal the true parts of ourselves by carving away all the muck that is not us. In the car driving away from the meeting, the preacher on my radio mentions David and Goliath. He talks about Jesus and where we put him in our car.

Well, this all seems very odd as I just heard David mentioned and now am driving my car. He goes on to ask his listeners, "Where do you put Jesus in your car? In the passenger seat? Do you force him to be a backseat driver? Or do you allow him front and center to take the wheel?" This struck me as an especially apropos idea as we are always taught in recovery to let our Higher Power take the proverbial wheel, learning that often our need to control has left us steering ourselves into ditches and on unruly roads, perhaps in the very worst of directions. Now he had my attention—but whoa, what was that?

There are bright blue lights whirring in my rearview mirror! Let me pull over and let that cop go and catch whatever bad guy has gotten their interest. Oops, they are after me. Huh. It has been decades since I have been stopped by a cop and it appears that a lot has changed since then. There are now alternating scalding white and blue lights, very confusing like an acid trip disco. And the sound! There is the familiar siren but perhaps more amplified, the high twirling whistle to alert the world of imminent danger, in this case, me.

But then, when I can't pull over because there is no shoulder to the road, even though I slow down and use my right turn signal to indicate intention, the cop car uses an absolutely insulting, giant, scraping, fart-like noise. It sounds kind of like that sound from Family Feud when he says, "Survey says," and then there is this loud, almost embarrassing "Eeeeeeehhhhhhhh!!!" indicating that you guessed a wrong answer. But it's even more grating and disagreeable, like "You have definitely FAILED at driving! Eeeeeeehhhhhhh!!!! Get your ass off the road now. Eeeeeeehhhh!! for the way you maneuver your car." And so I go onto the grass.

A Girl-With-the-Dragon-Tattoo-looking female cop comes to my passenger side window as I search for my registration from the glove compartment, whose door just falls open creating the impression of havoc, which the officer eagerly examines for signs of something. She only asks for my license which she quickly checks, then turns to me to ask, "Ma'am, do you know why I pulled you over tonight?"

"I have no idea," I reply honestly.

"Have you been drinking tonight?"

I laugh. "Not a drop in five years!"

She asks to approach the driver's side window, unimpressed, and rephrases, "Ma'am, have you consumed any alcoholic beverages this evening?"

"I just came from a meeting." Now I am giving her my serious face.

She sizes me up and explains why she stopped me. "You were swerving all over the road, both over the dotted white line and the double yellow and you accelerated from twenty-five to fifty-five miles per hour in a very short period of time."

Patting my old Passat proudly, I suddenly hear the VW motto in my head, "Drivers Wanted," then tap my speedometer like maybe it's broken. "Huh, cuz I really thought I only got up to about fifty, maybe fifty-two, the limit there was forty-five mph so that's not so bad. And as for the swerving, I'm very sorry; I was eating some french fries."

She seems satisfied at my directness and shines her flashlight on my passenger seat which has fries dumped into a burger box and ketchup in its adjoining compartment, obviously having been recently swiped through. "Okay ma'am, be safe."

"Thank you and I'll be more careful." My words dissipate into her retreating bounds as she turns and walks briskly back to her car, her radio squawking an alert of something perhaps more promisingly deviant than me.

The next day my spiritual friend, Peter mentions David and Goliath. In my heart and mind I shout into the sky, with upward turned head and skyward glance, "What, God??!!"

How am I not 'letting Jesus take my wheel'?

I ruminate a bit on Michelangelo's David. He made a very big impression on me when I saw him in Florence and I kept a picture of him on my wall for years, but I don't think I was in any way cognizant of exactly why, besides the obvious. All I know is that something in his chiseled perfection channeled down deep to something in my core, and we all know it is not his endowment. It was not his perfectly rippling abs either, though I do remember wondering what it might be like to touch his real-man-version's thighs; would they be hairy? Hard to tell. I was interested in the smoothness of him and the rightness, the all-in-place-ness and serenity in his stare.

Historians say it is obvious that he is in motion, that the torque of his body and cock of his head imply movement and make the marble come to life. There is the beauty of that moment between conscious choice and action. But it is the stillness that strikes me. And perhaps the assuredness. He is going up against some mammoth foe, who is not even deemed worthy of representation in Michelangelo's piece, armed only with a slingshot and he is still. He is calm.

Sobriety is like that. If you had told a younger me that she would not be drinking in a couple of years, it would have felt like lifting a steamroller with my pinky finger. Sometimes an action as seemingly small as hurling a tiny stone into the air, propelled only by a flimsy leather strap can seem as momentous as stopping the steaming locomotive of my life on booze, or as protecting the civil liberties of the Republic of Florence (as David was a symbol of when he was created), defeating those demons embodied as giants.

But it is most important to remember that none of it is possible alone. As David knew. His confidence and faith gave more prominent power than those six little stones in his pocket. He states that God kept his sheep safe against bears and lions so he would be safe from some Philistine giant named Goliath. That is the ultimate litmus of perfect surrender, willingness to let "Jesus take the wheel". That faith and relinquishing to the divine is what I need to become more of the masterpiece version of myself, otherwise, in my haste or carelessness, my simple willfulness, doubt and fear, I shall chip off say, the glorious shoulder of my blossoming version of David.

NEPAL VERSUS NOW

Memory: Kathmandu, January 2015

Northfield Hotel

Breathe in; breathe out. I hear junkies in ruckus on the streets, coughing up Kathmandu debris, hankering for a hunk a' that brown sugar, black tar, heroin. I can feel it in the rustling air, the restless honks the light cars emit in the night, the yelling, the slurring, and the anxious busting at the seams.

I am sober. And nothing feels more right.

Earlier this evening, two wobbly brown men muttered through their creased faces with ashy voices, "You want a little smoke?" I said, "No, but enjoy."

The discordant yearning builds. There are drumbeats, live bands and a man yelling in Nepali for his drug of choice, the twitch in the air a palpable need that only ever gets revised, rewritten into an expansion of ever-greater proportion.

But I don't want to rewrite this feeling, alone in this room in a moderate guest house, just right, at ease in my skin, without need of expansion. I nestle into the soft warmth of my comfy bed, in the red glow of the electric heater, surrounded by fleshy, satiny pink wallpaper, roiling in shine and finish.

Two Weeks Later

I had been helping in the gem store of my Kathmandu hotel while I waited for Nanda to return to his village to supposedly say goodbye to his family. He had returned a darkened, weathered stranger to me and we were to fly home to America the next day and prepare for our wedding. I hadn't slept in four nights and I believe I was in an altered state of consciousness, honestly not knowing if I was awake or half asleep.

Then something real and moving appeared to be burrowing in the crevice where wall hit ceiling and I was sucked into it—as if I were melting into the reality that all molecules are one and all that is needed to be in any other element is the consciousness of it. I started out being a part of the silver rings I had been helping to package for the owner of the Northfield Hotel. It's as if I were sinking down into the metal that composed them, then weaving around myself and merging flawlessly into other rings as if that were always possible. The giant worm in the ceiling belying the existence of reality. Too confusing. Merging with the All. How to describe it.

In trancelike blur, I can't tell which way I will go—toward the choice that matter is believable and particles are

Nepal Versus Now

distinct and separate from us or back to that other side—
the thing that is pushing through the ceiling, some force
calling me to become what we really are, quantum physics
particles of one great thing, the same thing. Which one is
real? I'm stuck between sleep and awake in this painful
stretching and shrinking. I can't stop. I am expanding and
contracting like continuous oceanic breaths, back and
forth.

At one point I'm a table's leg, spinning through fibers,
embodying splinters, then I am the hotel that holds
the table. In another instant, I am the very sheet that is
covering me, then I melt through it–up and through and
into the All, the More, the whole Universe and I desperately seek to find the way back; to anchor myself
in definition, the place that tells my story, where I am
in Kathmandu and preparing to bring back and marry
a Nepali man I'm not even sure I like. Where there is
fear that I am crazy--broken, in need of Codependents
Anonymous, Sex and Love Addicts Anonymous, EMDR
(that tapping, reprogramming therapy), and one of those
white jackets. I have been up for four nights, wallowing in
uncertainty.

All of it seems so small and unimportant now because it's
just the story–the means by which to pin down a cloud,
as if otherwise I would float away and be lost. I have to
be pinned down. I'll take it. I'll take my story. It's not so
serious.

Oops, I picked the wrong story. Result: a bigamist husband
who will return to his village to satisfy his mother's wishes
that he marry a Nepali girl, even after he has vowed

forever to me, in front of gods, my friends and family, a priest, and Sita, our officiator.

The present; On my way to a first date after the bigamy:

Driving to my first romantic encounter after I have received proof of my husband's marriage to another woman I find myself full from a letter I just received in the mail from Tim. He was the owner of Swordplay fencing studio in L.A. where I worked in for five years. I had been interested in becoming a pirate for children on the weekends (after studying fencing at the American Academy of Dramatic Arts with him) but instead became part of a fight team. We studied Olympic fencing, stage combat with many different weapons and prepared to be a major Hollywood force. I was more enamored with the wisdom Tim offered, his integrity and focus. I taught classes, did all the event coordinating for three years, performed as a pirate at birthday parties for kids, did extravagant swordfights for events like the opening of the Long Beach Aquarium. It was exhilarating to be near him. He led from knowing that to be behind a sword means everything you are is on the line, that you are willing to risk death for your beliefs. He proved that by being the best father to his daughter, Carolanne, that I have ever witnessed. He put me in a Disney movie, a national Nike commercial, and two swordplay training films for actors. I could have been his protégé.

He threw down the gauntlet. And I failed to pick it up. Because of booze. He invited me to be his grasshopper, to train with him privately early in the morning and I didn't show up. I carried that failure for years until recently I wrote him an amends letter. Months passed and I assumed he crumpled the letter and tossed it into his wastebasket with a flick of his wrist, swatting away the fly I'd become to him. Then I received his response. He did not remember my failure, only me, fondly.

He said, "I am proud of you for having beaten the booze. These things are not easy and most people have no idea how to defeat a demon. I think that if we are wise and not ashamed of what has happened and what has scared us, we come out on the other side of it stronger than we could have ever been without it. I think these things are tests and challenges that we either pass or fail and I do understand how difficult it is and that makes me respect you more than I ever have."

The words seep through me and melt the failure like a June sun. I am driving to a date, a new prospect in the wake of my husband's only recently discovered bigamy. There could be so much tenderness, so much vulnerability, but it doesn't matter. I am fine.

I am soaring now, down the grade and singing some pop God song about shining your light. I stick my hand out the window to let it dance with the wind in absolute exaltation of being alive. I have no sorrow and I feel tears warm my face as I totally and suddenly realize that this triumph is the most important thing in my life; it is a treasure I nurture with hard work and continued searching. Nothing else matters–that I don't have a kid or a Prince Charming, that I haven't published at age fourteen like I planned, that I left a restaurant I opened in New York City to flood and rot. This is what I have to write about.

THE PERFECTION OF EVERYTHING

Journal: Freak Street, Nepal, 2013

Sometimes it hits me all at once, the perfection of everything.

The view from this craggy little corner of the world, staring out the window of this little café, which brings to mind Hemingway's "clean, well-lighted place," at a yellow cement building, windows boarded up, white pigeon dropping splatters dotting the awning like a Pollock, shops below; a T-shirt printer/embroiderer sports Buddha Eyes and Everest caps, next door is Freak Street Namaste Beads with malas and other prayer stuffs drooped languorously from wall-to-wall, every inch of the ten square-foot purple-walled shop laced in beauty, multicolored round beads, scarves, faded, waving in the light to caress the morning air with rainbows.

Above, a white stucco building sports drying laundry; towels, exotic print bedsheets, a jacket and shirts, even the tattered plastic burlap sack clinging to the empty flagpole seems useful. Outside my window where I drink hot ginger-lemon tea with honey are two plants cluttered with cigarette butts; and even that seems perfect as sunlight spackles the faded street where tourists and locals saunter slowly by.

Earlier that day, the darkness slowly peeled away like an Indian virgin revealing her shoulders, scored by a symphony of slowly building gongs. People greeted their gods in the many temples around the town's square, bringing plates of marigolds and other offerings to anoint statues with as they bow, shoeless in the freezing morning chill. They spatter oils at tomb-shrouded figures, prayers violently streaming from fingers of prostrated forms. Gong gong, then birds' songs, from the soft rumble of pigeons' warbling coos, nesting, mating, to morning birds gathered on a rooftop, a soft cacophony of high-pitched trill, heavenly larks of the daylight.

On cue, a dog barks; there are so many, limping, mangy, fighting, afraid; I have to ignore their sad eyes because without hundreds of tons of dog food and shelters, I can do nothing. The soft bristle of the brooms as purple and turquoise, maroon and navy-outfitted women diligently sweep at the town square's debris, ash and trash, smoldering recklessness from the day before disappearing into care and meticulousness.

My meltdown and puppy tracks. I am leaving work at noon after working all night, not having been able to sleep some days in a row. I am unwoven by the atrocities of my mind. Did I screw up? Did I overstep my bounds? A client has wanted her files sealed for legal reasons. Her counselor is on leave and I emailed the new director-boss, and left in fear of once again being called a boundary over-stepper for simply trying to cover the bases. I am just a tech, a "Chemical Dependency Technician" and I know that is nothing, but still I want to help the suffering addicts and am given conflicting instructions. There are then critical comments of another tech who tells me basically to stay out of it. This is a toxic environment with gossip, and moves like a chessboard to avoid blame, avoid HIPPA violations, stay in the box.

Then it all tumbles down when my mom leaves some message about how I need to ask for a two-week vacation. She suggests I take some time off my new job and come heal at the beach when I do not have the ability to do that. All dissolves, it crumbles, thin walls of sanity demolished in seconds as I think-scream to her, "I can't! I am not good like you! I am not accomplished with a Ph.D., a working professional who honors herself and can make demands on this world. Take all that you are that was bad and that was shameful and a mistake and put it into a paper cup, like on a subway or in the garbage, and that is me! Don't you get it??!! Don't you understand? I have failed! I have missed the boat. I was deemed special and possible and glorious and pretty once, full of potential until all that melted away with mistakes, with my drinking, my wasted choices, the full-on crazy mishegoss of all that bad stuff in the paper cup becoming the adult me. The blurred lines and the crooked unfinished corners, your deepest regrets, that became me. I made all the wrong moves and traveled down a long and corroding spiral to the bottom of the hole which is here, where a husband had to leave me because I was so crazy and am nothing to no one and am not even good enough to help at my job where I am hidden in the night to work!"

Oh yeah. That's it. I just remembered why this is happening. She had the baby and it was a boy. I can't divorce him for three more months (N.C. dictates I wait a year after physical separation) but I just found out my husband, who is still my husband, had the reward of a lifetime for leaving me and marrying her. He had a boy. He had a boy four days ago. And this is what is happening to me. So this is shadow.

Then I look up as it is raining softly and that is a good thing to wake one up, especially out of a bad reverie, and somehow I am walking my mom's puppy that I have for a month while she travels in Canada and the tears and the rain are all blurred together and there he is, this sleek black, compact streamline of muscle and wag just bounding into the air snipping at a butterfly too high to bite, but it keeps trying anyway. His black shiny body springing up with all that he is, just flinging himself toward the gray fuzzy flutter. And it stops me in my tracks.

And I laugh. So hard. This puppy doesn't care that I have been abandoned or have not earned notoriety or own the house we sleep in. This puppy doesn't care about HIPPA or lines or obeying the rules. This puppy is so immersed in the beauty of the now that I must be too. The purple violets on the ground beckon me to remember Kathmandu at 5:00 a.m., chai, serenity from calamity. The perfection of everything.

Goodbye

When my husband and I had settled in Saluda, North Carolina, I started what I thought to be my dream job, Chemical Dependency Technician to drunks and addicts. I thought my sobriety and work ethic were the right combination to excel in this recovery profession but instead was rejected for six day positions and clearly shown that this was not the right place or career for me. But my desire to do service grows and after working there for a year and a half I resigned to transition into elder care. This was my last night at Pavillion, International in Mill Spring:

October 2015

I am shaking a little bit as I fill my water bottle for one of the last times, perhaps from the giddiness of goodbye. How could I be so sad after eating a meal with my coworker Delta, who publicly despises me and has apparently been responsible for my inability to get a day job here? How could I be so attached to Jennifer, the typically-Western-North-Carolina obese one? She loves Sundrop soda and tells funny stories. She made waves for me after I tried to help her get remote computer access, she said I was intrusive. I asked about her conversation with a shy nurse who came out of his shell with her. I was so curious that I revealed my demon spawn pushy side, apparently overstepping bounds to pry into their secret conversation.

And how could I be so attached to these addicts, these drunks, these liars and thieves as even now one comes down the hall telling me he can't stop thinking about using even though he was in jail just before this and didn't use for a while. I am not supposed to be personal and relate to them too much but I do it anyway. I have been scolded for these "porous boundaries" of mine which don't stop me as I reach out to him, remind him that he does not need to worry about the future. He is fretting about taking too many sleep meds in the wake of his detox and how that will impact his life when he gets home. I tell him to just focus on the important work he has on hand right now one day at a time.

How can I have such deep love and affection for these lost souls, the princess who complained that she couldn't sleep with the humidifier on in the room with princess number two who couldn't sleep without it because her nose was so stopped up and she couldn't breathe. They are still both here; I am surprised there hasn't been a room change, their spoiledness was not commended, but they are still roommates and are both sleeping now with no humidifier. Princess number one won out.

How can I even love them a smidgeon when I have been vituperated beyond recognition for things that were not quite done, or interpreted incorrectly, or out-and-out made up?! How can I? But when I open the door a crack on their sleeping forms, knowing this skinny leathered one from my sober community in Hendersonville, who still, to this day cannot stay sober. She has been asking for sugar-free nicotine gum to avoid the one calorie in the regular; This one has just arrived and is not participating in any of the programs, explicit in her sleeping on top of the bed with her own, fluffy blue blanket; or this one who smells nice, like the orange ginger I remember so well from New York, Sabon's signature smell, so healthy, nurturing and spiritual.

When I crack the doors open upon them, my heart cracks too, just a little. In bond, in recognition, in defiance, and in glory! As well it does at the prospect of leaving these sticky, these tricky, these also vituperating coworkers.

I guess I know that at the end of the day we are all the same. And I don't just mean in the recovery way, where one drunk alone can communicate with another and there is an inexplicable bond, a sisterhood and a brotherhood beyond bounds, although that be true. I mean in a real human sense.

Perhaps I am getting older. Leaving used to be easier. Never flawless, though. I recall when I studied at Oxford, for a summer abroad program through UNC. It was perhaps the most ecstatic social experience of my life. I had never fit in anywhere so seamlessly. I was loved by every single member of that study abroad group–I could talk to the intellectuals and help make them feel included; I could hang with Lucy the now world-famous pianist. I could party with the frat boys, stupid Stuey being my sometimes beau for at least the season of that study abroad summer where the common laws of DKE segregation did not touch him, did not discolor his innate preferences. And there were artists and weirdos and freaks alike; the ones I could secretly relate to the most. The saying goodbye was like butter melting over hot corn on the cob, simply dripping to the floor. Perhaps because there was enough butter in the world and enough butter on my corn. But as you get older, you begin to cut carbs, watch your billowing waist, your cholesterol, your sugar, your fats. All of it. And in life it becomes more serious, more complicated, harder to part with.

The decision to go away from here was a no-brainer, accepting perhaps a worse job to move from this dead-end one, this vampire shift, dreaming that my calling was in recovery–that my heart longed to be a part of this process, this healing, this bit of work called rehab. But now I question whether it has been a nightmare? A daydream? A complete confusion of passions infused by my own process of recovery which, though it feels so solid, so flourishing, so free and inspiring, has only been occurring for around four years and eight months which is relatively little in recovery standards. They call it "early recovery" like I am a baby, still learning how to walk, how to bathe and feed myself, not quite at the phase where I can play well with others, which is true I guess. But I grieve this loss harder, this misplaced building of a foundation toward a something that will never be. Who knows what cards God has up her sleeve for me?

The goodbye aches. The quivering in my stomach runs through my skin, my pores feel sad. As I reach the change of shift and my cue to be gone forever the staunch one cries. She looks over my shoulder as I clock out on the computer for the very last time and tears drip from her ruddy skin, her dried apple-wrinkled face. I broke, a little, a lot? Like with an egg, if you crack it, the entrails spill out onto the pan. Her goodbye cracks my heart a little like that, knowing I will probably never see her again.

Then there is the one who is the hardest to say goodbye to. Another third shift tech who preaches at his church in Spartanburg. He already has a full time career there, but has to work nights now to pay for his daughter's college because her Pell Grants disappeared. We discussed the parable of David and Goliath, as it kept popping up for me. He told me how much it meant to him and that what stood out for him and he would highlight in his sermons was a small and often overlooked detail that David had shared food with the soldiers. He felt like that was a secret, underlying meaning, pointing us toward service. On one of my last nights he said, "I'm really gonna miss our fireside chats." And that is true, the moments in the middle of the night which sustain you are somehow more profound, more surreal like the Twilight Zone–leaving an impression by daylight as if highlighted.

And if she hated me, Delta, whose name means change, if she really and truly wanted me to suffer, be ashamed, not be happy, then she wouldn't have brought back that present she'd given me and then taken home–the red, shiny coffee cup. She brought it back my last night. She secretly loves me and is worthy of the prayers I offer up on her behalf.

We are all the same. I trust God. I am cleaning house. I wish to help others, in whatever form that takes.

Gigi's Funeral

Shortly after I finalized my divorce, February, 2016, my grandmother, Gigi died. I went to Maryland for the funeral. My father's family had been scary and distant for me as I never even once shared any time with them with my father while I was growing up. It was my mother who stayed close to Gigi, even after she and he were divorced. She took me to visit her many times through the years. I knew her as a bigger than life, elegant queen, and always felt I was probably just a little bit too shabby to be a part of her world. But here I am, in the end, sitting on my cousin's couch, having a vivid memory:

It was a hot summer night and I was at my dad's house in Zebulon, North Carolina. I have dreamt that I was excruciatingly thirsty. I have gone to the bathroom repeatedly to drink from the little plastic rinse cup which resides in the toothbrush holder. As I gulped thirstily from it, I could not get quenched. I saw a hole in the bottom of the cup which was draining the precious liquid before it could reach my lips.

I am awake and my father is comforting me, maybe years later, "There, there, everything is okay," patting my back.

As the last of my grandparents, Gigi's passing sort of cements a deal, the terms of which are encoded to me, but something has become final—official. We are both meditating, my father and I, in the wake of the dying, amongst paintings of an owl, a sailboat, and my great-grandfather's original work. It is a painting of Daddy Lew in a blackened alley. He is wearing a London-looking black overcoat and walking away from us, I presume to go for a drink, into some dark, speakeasy-looking unmarked door. I found out recently that my great-grandfather, Lew Lehr, was a hopeless alcoholic and suffered from tremendous depression.

I had only hitherto known him as a famous star, reciting Movietone News and Monkey Show comedy, a representation of the world in which I was not good enough to partake. The only color in the entire painting is a sprig of holly in a trashcan across the alleyway from the speakeasy door, its joy in vast contrast to his world of muck. I can relate.

The wind swoops up to caress me and rustle the leaves outside the window, and as always, I know that this is God. But this time I feel my grandmother hovering above us saying, "This is nice. Everything is okay."

I remember her lavish life, plush antique dolls and all those silver articulated fish atop her coffee table, by fancy velvet furniture, silver horsehair brushes, gilded mirrors. It seems impossible that all that is gone, faded into memories and perhaps a few dusty boxes in someone's attic.

Gigi's Funeral

A tear rolls down my cheek as I envision Gigi the way I remember her: wide and full of pomp and makeup, fluffy hair and cooing voice like a sweet pigeon saying, "Yes, yes." My arms around her prominent neck and her smile plastered to eternity. She coos on in the wind and whispers that this is my inheritance, and to take it into my heart. I have this unclaimed legacy and I should cement it in with the love and acceptance I received from my barely known relatives. Two relatives started the successful Under Armour company, another was a minor league baseball star, Matt Coenen, whose face stares back at me from a baseball card as I write this. My great grandmother, Gigi's mother, was a Vaudevillian star, Anna Leonhardt. My grandmother herself was the first female talk show host in America. I am proud.

She says to take this into my heart as my inheritance, my due right. Things fade, pride vanishes, accomplishments disintegrate into the dust of light that they've always been. But knowing who you are, that never dies.

Trish

Today one of the biggest treasures of my life is to be a sponsor to others. Trish is a long-term sponsee. She has given me permission to share her story in hopes that it will help others.

We are sitting at Umi, our favorite girls' luncheon place. While other alcoholics nurse waters or old-folk, discounted value dishes at Denny's post meeting, we enjoy a full, four-course bento box or sushi at this Japanese haven. She is big, but not by choice, by cirrhosis and survival. And she is beautiful, with frizzy, salt and pepper-hair, always elegantly adorned in local thrift stores' grandest flowing fabrics and jewels (with a sundry of matching purses).

She has finally made a year sober and is now eligible for a new liver, or perhaps even hers has regenerated enough to not need one. Her new look on life is already apparent and I thank Goddess every day I have gotten to be some small part of it. By grace she is alive and our relationship is one of the most important I have found. I am honored and touched to sponsor her, to walk with her on this journey and be the recipient of this time at these luncheons which she claims to look forward to all week. I remember that feeling in my early, tumultuous sobriety in New York. While other New York City alcoholics resorted to the Galaxy diner for discounted ice cream and bad coffee, my sponsor Abby and I exclusively dined at Pigalle French Bistro after my women's meeting on Saturdays.

This week Trish says, "Wow, I guess you actually don't know a lot about me."

I laugh at her slow discovery of her own guardedness. She has told me her secrets but not much of her life.

"Well, one of the many times I tried to stop drinking, I had stopped for that day and I figured out in my head that I needed to go and expose how much I drank. And so I filled up this plastic lawn garbage bag with bottles, all of it was Heineken and vodka back then. I just realized that I needed to expose myself and my problem. So I bagged them all and dragged it out to the main highway down two roads.

When I got to Archer Road, I saw that there was a dump truck and it was on and I saw that it was goin. So I got into the dump truck and tried to figure out how to drive it. There were lots and lots of knobs. So this person came out and asked what was I doing. I guess he was the dump truck driver. I told him I had to drag these bottles down. Then he asked me if there was anyone I could call and I told him about this clubhouse with a bunch of meetings called Triangle Club and he called. He told me he had family members that had my problem. He asked me if it was all right to pray with him and I said yes.

Trish

After a while, the guy from Triangle club came. And he was an Elvis impersonator. He drove a yellow Cadillac, a piece of junk, but it was still a Cadillac. The license plate spelt out Elvis. He came and he threw the big garbage bag full of empty bottles in the trunk of the Cadillac and drove me down to the Triangle Club. And then he tossed the bag of bottles into the dumpster. He didn't say a word to me–I just came in and I sat down and I waited for a meeting.

When I got a ride back from the meeting, I went to bed that night and all of a sudden I heard all this noise and singing, with a band and everything. And all of a sudden there was a white light in the corner of my trailer bedroom and I went outside and I heard music and voices and I tried to follow them and I spent all night trying to find the voices. I went through the woods trying to find the voices. I went to the 7:00 a.m. meeting and I believed there were little tiny hidden cameras there and they were tape recording me as one of the worst drunks in the world and making a movie on how if I could get sober, anybody could get sober. And I was the star of this documentary about women in recovery.

Then I got home and I started hearing the voices again, and so I still thought it was God talking to me and because I was slipping deeper into the DTs, I started walking into the part of the neighborhood which was paved, where the more normal people lived and I was looking for God and these people were building this little house. They had just bought this little house and they were rebuilding it. And I said I had lost God and did she know anything about it, and she looked at me real funny. So I changed what I said and asked her if she had seen my dog. She just looked at me real weird again and asked her husband to come out. So I left and went back to the trailer, and I was still hearing all this music and singing, so I tried to chase after it. I went to the deep woods and I was barefooted. And I found a house; I came upon a house. And it was barred shut with the metal bars that kinda looked churchy-looking and I thought God was inside. So I sat down on the porch and I started–I decided I was gonna tell God in the house my fourth step (the fourth of the twelve steps is where you take a 'thorough and fearless inventory of yourself' which you then recite to a sponsor as a fifth step) so I started on and on, I was rambling on what I thought was a fourth step. Then very slowly this face came around the corner of the house and he asked me if I was all right. And I said I was just doin' a fourth step. He was a fireman, they had the fire department, I don't know why, and there was a police car and a fireman…so they asked me questions that I can't remember, but I still thought I was in this wonderful movie. But they wanted me to get in the ambulance.

We went to the hospital and as we drove there, I was starin' at all the metal things and I thought these were all the cameras and equipment to make my film. So I got to the hospital and they wanted me to pee in a cup and I just couldn't. So I put water from the water fountain in the cup and gave it to the guy…so they knew. Then they took me to the crisis center. And they asked me if I had a history of schizophrenia and I said no. Then they asked me if I heard voices and I said no because the film was supposed to be a secret. Then I went to the crisis unit. On the way there, I was still thinking that everything was a big film and that I could go behind the sets and see everything, but it was still a big secret and I heard a voice and it was God, it said how it was a film and stuff. And I just saw there were a bunch of camera guys. And I went into my room and watched a film of my daughter being horrendously abused by her father, and at the end there was a picture of her and her father and I realized she was fine. And I realized that all my fears were basically unfounded. Then I went out into the common area and the voices started to fade away and I was really unhappy that the voices faded away. And I went and told the doctor everything and he explained delirium tremens to me. He pointed out someone in the common room who was talking to himself and just walking around and mumbling and he said, 'do you know what a wet brain is?' and pointed at him. I was one step away from going into a mental hospital for a six month evaluation–I mean I was this close. Just thinking about it makes me really shaky on the inside, what lengths alcoholism, you know, how it can take a person down, took me down to such a degree, and still I kept drinking after that. When they released me, I managed to stay sober for about three weeks. That was pretty good for me. And I went to meetings while I was drinking. I kept going to meetings even while I was drinking and I think it helped a lot."

"Wow," I say, because what else is there?

I do not take any credit for this transformation from a believed-psychotic woman to a sane and sober lady who lunches, dressed in flowing fabrics, picking delicately at her sushi, giving me an Italian sheep's wool hat for Christmas.

No, this is how it works, apparently. I think back to the day when I was soul-bereft and thought myself condemned to a lifetime of failure to stop my drinking, trapped in a prison of repetitive self-torture.

Every morning toward the end I would swear, "Not today, I hurt too much. I won't drink today." And by the end of my crazy, chaotic overwhelming New York City restaurant day, or, oh hell, it could have been a smooth and mundane one just as easily, there I would be at the BLT bar stool talking to Andrew the bartender like I was a wine snob. Drinking bottomless crystal goblets of red wines, forgetting to order dinner before the kitchen closed, and then babbling incoherently to a cab driver as if I were his marriage counselor.

Then when I went into the program there was Abby. Day one. The only one who really held onto me, in a sea of numbers flying at my face, weird women asking me what my plan was, telling me I had to go to ninety meetings in ninety days and that I couldn't have lamb chops with the perfect pinot noir today, but that tomorrow I could, because it was a one day at a time thing. Then Abby gave me her number on a card and said, "Dial it, don't file it." She texted me later that day, at 5:45. "How ya doin?"

And that first sober day when I couldn't sleep in the middle of the night, I called her. I had never reached out in all my life to another human being like that. In despair. Lost. Needing help. She told me to fluff my pillow; that's where the bad dreams lay. Flip it over and try to rest, that's what her mother had told her. I'll never forget it. When I thanked her and told her she was saving my life, she simply texted back, "That's how we do."

One of the wise women in my sober community has regaled me with a story about Trish in her first days in the area, trying to quit drinking unsuccessfully. She says she was conned into picking up a neighbor of Trish's when she was at a meeting once. Her house was twenty-five miles out of town. My friend picked her up and with her came Trish, looking dilapidated and comatose. And my friend recalls thinking to herself, "Man, if she can do it, then anyone can."

Bookend Two

As I stretch in the shower today, it is a whole different story. Visions of my morning prayer and meditation readings echo in my mind; how God says ego can neither be qualified as good or bad, as it is relative, necessary for us to pin ourselves down in this world which is not defined, but is absolute, that it is the ego that reminds us so in its uncanny, crinkled assertion that we are separate, that we are individuating, that we should strive to be special. Another morning prayer book said to be close to your own soul, as that is the gateway to allowing more of God in, an innate friendship with yourself, an ability to know and take care of you.

Today I worked at a retirement community, helping to bring dignity and love to them in sprigs of possible. I am training as a Med Tech. I am signed up to become a CNA. I have three sponsees and three sponsors. I go to four meetings a week and spend an hour a day writing a deeper step four than I ever imagined possible, taking personal inventory, literally finding the things of the past that no longer serve me, and learning to see them so I can ask the Spirit of the Universe to remove them. I have been invited into a women's writing circle by my next-door neighbor.

I live in a luxurious mountain lodge with two king-size beds, a huge deck, and a fireplace.

I lean against the back wall of my glamorously fancy and clean bathroom shower laced in browns and golds, gilded by marble and antique pheasant faucet and handles. I stretch. I extend my left leg back into the steamy pellets of gentle pour which massage my aching calf muscle and I push into health. I feel layers of light little droplets of God's love because I am willing. They trickle onto the tendon that had shrunken up; that feeble, weary casing of a muscle pounded upon by years of walking ceaselessly on concrete, tile, marble, and wood floors, those booming steps of supposed progress toward restaurant perfection (never happens), beating my poor body into a pulpified state of you-think-you-should, and now I am healing.

With time away and this deliberate stretch marking a ritual of loving that was prescribed to me years ago by this god sent podiatrist named Brian in downtown Manhattan, who admitted that although he should probably prescribe some invasive and expensive career-glorifying surgery—he knew from tried and true years of long treatment, mostly of runners who could barely walk whom he had helped to run again within months—that the best method was simply practicing these stretches.

When I first was given this prescription, I was actively drinking. The importance of doing these exercises faded into the tight crevices of denial like so many patches of thoughts and should-dos and would-bes, like eating breakfast, getting a checkup, doing anything positive for myself because working in the restaurant business took all of me. The only reason I was willing to go to this foot doctor was that I simply could no longer walk. I was limping around as the hunch-footed restaurant manager of the largest outdoor café in Manhattan where emergencies happened all the time, which meant that I would traverse the equivalent length of an Olympic pool in seconds.

Once, for example, to tend to my poor server who collapsed from dehydration. Once to break up a bar fight. And another time to get stir sticks from a retail store to preclude the ensuing onslaught of many spoonless coffees served during a dishwasher crisis—stuff like that. When I agreed to this prescription, I fully intended to do the stretches, like he said, three times a day, but managed in reality to only do it in the shower.

It was all the time and energy I had, thus the earlier realization that something was vastly wrong with my life as it was—out of control, unmanageable and that somehow I was at the heart of the disturbance.

Today my experience is a far cry from that day in the winter of 2010 when the floodgate burst and the tears overwhelmed that former me. I like to imagine a silver thread connecting today to then—arching over time, growth, and change, increasing its distance between the bookend of that day when I fell apart in the shower to the bookend of today, this moment of clarity and recovery. They are solid and they are real but they can constantly be in flux, expanding to accommodate change, breadth of experience, and recovery. The more space between the bookends the merrier, as distance accentuates the progress, but even more importantly, the relief. And in that space lays tremendous gratitude. I remember what it felt like to be trapped in the prison of my routine with alcohol, the wanting it, the pretending I didn't, the inevitable caving into it on a daily basis like succumbing to an irresistibly seductive lover, one who'd been licking his fingers all day in ravenous anticipation of my downfall—awaiting my crumble into his arms where I tried to pretend I wanted to be, but really was powerless to avoid, and in hell when there.

The space between now and Bookend One, where my journey began, grows broader and more spacious with every breath I take. And I do so now. And all I have is gratitude. As I emerge from the sticky tar pit of that lost place, that hellhole which was worsened the most by my own denial, feeling that I had reached game over and totally lost this fugue state of life if I admitted I had to go into a program to heal my body, spirit, and soul.

My sobriety is my Ph.D. It is rare. It is precious. I will guard it with my life, God willing, one day at a time.

If I can do it, anyone can.

About the Author

Ali Cassandra Webster hails from Chapel Hill, North Carolina where she obtained dual Bachelor of Arts degrees in English and Dramatic Arts from the University of North Carolina at Chapel Hill.

A budding writer since twelve years old, Ali attended the prestigious Duke Young Writer's camp for five years graced by renowned Southern authors such as Lee Smith and Clyde Edgerton.

After college the lure of acting took over the drive to write and Ali moved to Los Angeles, California where she worked with a fencing studio in Burbank, opening the door to earning a living acting in commercials and a Disney film.

Soon tired of the LA lifestyle, she moved to New York City where she managed a successful restaurant. Working constantly, Ali's inner and outer worlds pressed hard upon her and became too much to bear. In a moment of clarity she left it all behind to go to India, which was the catalyst for redefining herself in peaceful, joyful, and gentle ways.

Today, Ali lives in the tranquil mountains of Western North Carolina and is thrilled to be back at the pen to share her journey with you.

www.ingramcontent.com/pod-product-compliance
Lightning Source LLC
Chambersburg PA
CBHW072017110526
44592CB00012B/1346